WAKE THE FUCK UP
A JOURNEY FROM DEATH TO AWAKENING

By

CAROL BANAYOS

Published in Canada

Copyright © 2016 - Carol Banayos

ALL RIGHTS RESERVED. No part of this publication may be reproduced, distributed or transmitted in any form or by any means, including photocopying, recording, or other electronic or mechanical methods, without the prior written permission of the publisher, except in the case of brief quotations embodied in critical reviews and certain other noncommercial uses permitted by copyright law. For permission requests, write to the publisher, addressed "Attention: Permissions Coordinator," at the email address below.

Name: Carol Banayos
Website: www.carolbanayos.com
Email: cb@carolbanayos.com

Ordering Information:
Quantity sales. Special discounts are available on quantity purchases by corporations, associations, and others. For details, contact the "Special Sales Department" at the email address above.

WAKE THE FUCK UP – Carol Banayos -1st Edition.

EBook ISBN: 978-0-9949434-1-5
Paperback ISBN: 978-0-9949434-0-8

"One thing we do know: Life will give you whatever experience is most helpful for the evolution of your consciousness."

Eckhart Tolle

TABLE OF CONTENTS

INTRODUCTION
1

CHAPTER 1
Near-Death Experiences and Rebirth
7

CHAPTER 2
Conscious Awareness
29

CHAPTER 3
Spirituality
49

CHAPTER 4
Personal Growth and Development
63

CHAPTER 5
Forgiveness, Self-Love, Self-Acceptance,
and Self-Respect
77

CHAPTER 6
Health, Veganism, and the Many Benefits of
Adopting a Plant-Based Diet
97

CHAPTER 7
Resilience and Inner Strength
113

CHAPTER 8
Breaking out of Conformity and Finding Your Passion and Purpose in Life
129

CHAPTER 9
Be Your Authentic Self
141

CHAPTER 10
Making Assumptions Causes Drama
147

CHAPTER 11
Struggle and Pain is Inevitable. Belief Is King
153

CHAPTER 12
Conquer Your Fears and Build the Right Type of Confidence
171

CHAPTER 13
You Are a Magnet
177

CONCLUSION
183

ACKNOWLEDGEMENTS

I would like to acknowledge my mother, Lucita, who has supported me and my dreams, always told me to do my best and to treat others with love, kindness, and compassion. I would also like to acknowledge my father, Pat, for helping me become resilient and strong during this journey.

I would also like to express my love to my siblings, Florence, Oliver, and Liezl along with my sister-in-law Lori, my niece Carmen, and my nephew Logan.

Likewise, I would like to extend my gratitude to my best friends Leslie, Heather, Jazz, Jerilyn, Sugz, Abby, and Audrey for their continued love and support. I am grateful towards John, Keith, Sonia, Dennis, Kate, Silver, Ekaterina, Kasia, Kavita, Osamede, Mary, and Mohneer.

Moreover, I would like to express my appreciation to the people who had such a profound and positive impact on my life. Through their coaching, mentoring, reading of their books, quotes, live events, videos, movies, and audio programs, I have been influenced deeply. Some great inspirations include Christine Ottawa, Ruth Stargardter,

Eckhart Tolle, Tony Robbins, Oprah, Tara Baldwin, Malcolm Galdwell, Darren Hardy, Loretta Boulard, Cam Page, Jean Ledoux, Lorraine Andree, Jennifer Morris, Bonnie Schroeder, Claude Bristol, and Albert Einstein.

However, one cannot leave out Abraham Lincoln, Russell Conwell, Earl Nightingale, Wallace Wattles, Scot Anderson, Delia Joseph, Napoleon Hill, Bob Proctor, Les Brown, Dale Carnegie, Martin Luther King, Steve Jobs, Ralph Waldo Emerson, Elbert Hubbard, Don Miquel Ruiz, William Shakespeare, Sonny Carroll, Ralph Marston, Pharrell Williams, James Allen, George Samuel Clason and Jim Rohn regarding their impact on the rest of the world. John Maxwell, Donald Trump, Viktor Frankl, Paulo Coelho, Jose Silva, Maxwell Maltz, Russell Simmons, Bruce Lee, Will Smith and Lao Tzu have positively influenced the world as well. While the philosophies of Paramahansa Yoganada, Esther and Jerry Hicks, Neale Donald Walsch, David Icke, Max Igan, Peter Joseph, Gary Yourofsky, Gary Francione, Shaun Monson, Kip Andersen, Brendon Burchard, Vishen Lakhiani, Grant Cardone and Matrix (the movie) will never go unnoticed.

Lastly and most importantly, I would like to thank and acknowledge my brother from another mother, Mubarak Nsekarije, a.k.a Mufusa. If I was able to see further, it was because I was able to stand on the shoulder of giants. Thank you for letting me stand on your shoulders, for keeping me accountable, for your kindness, and for sharing your wisdom. I am deeply blessed and grateful to have you in my life.

INTRODUCTION

This book takes you through my journey of awakening and conscious awareness; it describes the moment of realization, when I knew I had to break out of the box I had placed myself in. I needed to tear down the walls and build a new bridge to get me from where I was, to where I was destined to be. As you read this book, you will see my story unfold, how I gradually learned that what I was destined for was nothing less than greatness.

However, that is not where I stopped. In my book, I have also tried to describe and explain my journey as I finally woke the fuck up. However, your journey might be completely different from mine. You might find yourself relating to my story as you move along your journey. What I am referring to, is that there is no specific trajectory or lone pathway that will take you to the ultimate "goal," or towards enlightenment.

However, what you CAN find here is inspiration. Perhaps my story rouses you from the deep waves of sleep that roll over you time and time again, pulling you in deeper as you struggle to hold on to the world around you. If you manage to keep a stronghold over reality and refuse to let go, consider yourself as more successful than over fifty percent of the world's population. In fact, this is probably a highly underestimated statistic.

If you are already one of the lucky few who have managed to find the right direction and have started reeling down this path, my story might initially scare you. You might suddenly become more aware of the different struggles and hurdles that life throws in people's paths. This may make the journey of awakening, or coming to conscious awareness, even more daunting than it already is.

However, I want you to consider it as knowledge or perhaps even life lessons. As you read the book, I would like you to connect with mistakes made by another human being. Consider yourself lucky, it is always better to learn from the mistakes of others than to go around making those same mistakes yourselves. Not only will you save yourself the time and energy of making the same mistakes, but there might also be some valuable pieces of advice you can attain from these.

At the end of the day, what matters is the perspective that you hold when reading my story. Whether you take it as one massive book full of advice, it all depends on you whether you think of it as nonsense, or as just another casual read for you on the bus. You are free to make anything of it, free to take away anything from it, and free to think anything of it.

Before you begin reading my story and the various questions and pieces of advice that I have thrown in here and there, I want you to read the following few paragraphs. This can be seen as my meager attempt to wake you up: a nutshell of what I want to say, the main reason that I wrote this book, and more. Think of this as the initial jerk your mother would give to your shoulder when trying to wake you the fuck up for school every morning.

Take a look at the world around you and the lives that people are leading. Most people are asleep at the wheel of life and seem to be walking around as if they are nothing more than empty vessels. This is because people merely appear to be passive recipients of what life throws at them. Like puppets on a drawstring, an external hand decides their every movement, what they say, what they do, how they feel... In fact, do they even feel anything in this state? One would, perhaps, consider it apt to describe them as lifeless zombies.

If that does not resonate with you, think of it this way. Have you ever daydreamed? Maybe you've done it while sitting at the desk in your office, waiting for the clock to strike five so you can be off, or maybe when you begin your endless commute home from work on the bus or when you are driving home from work. Most of us have daydreamed from time to time, if not every day. When we daydream, we feel like we are in another world altogether, it could be one where you are doing something completely different from your boring accountancy job, or maybe it is a world in which you are a different person altogether. Do you see yourself on your CEO's seat or with greater worldly gains than what you already have? Regardless of what you are daydreaming about, you and I all go through the exact same feeling: the feeling of losing touch with the world that we are actually living in. Do not be surprised if you completely forget who you are or where you are for those few moments.

However, there always comes a time in people's life when they are forced to finally wake up from this trance that they have been living in and take charge of their lives, as opposed to just letting life happen to them. Usually, this awakening comes about through an ah-ha moment or a tragic event. Once this happens, it is imperative for the old self to die if the new person is to grow.

It all begins by waking up from your sleep and becoming consciously aware: aware of who you are meant to be, what you are meant to be doing, and what your ultimate purpose is in this play of life.

My purpose in writing and sharing my story is to help people and to let them know that they are not alone in their journey of awakening: becoming consciously aware.

CHAPTER 1

Near-Death Experiences and Rebirth

"Death is not the greatest loss in life. The greatest loss is what dies inside us while we live."
Norman Cousins

The term "near-death experience" (NDE) was coined in 1975 in the book *Life After Life* by Raymond Moody, MD. A near-death experience (NDE) is a distinct subjective experience that people sometimes report after a near-death episode. In a near-death episode, a person is either clinically dead, near death, or in a situation where death is likely or expected. These circumstances include serious illness or injury, such as a car accident, military combat, childbirth, or suicide attempt. People in profound grief, in deep meditation, or just going about their normal lives have also described experiences that seem just like NDEs, even though these people were not near death. Many near-death experiencers (NDErs), meaning people who have experienced a near-death situation, have said the term "near-death" is not correct; they are sure that they were *in* death, not just *near* death.

From the stories I have heard about near-death experiences, whether those experiences were tragic or blissful, I feel that going through such an experience has resulted in a feeling of being reborn for most people. This feeling of being reborn is to have a second chance at life, to be able to look at life through different eyes, and to be given a fresh chance to live life to the fullest.

I can honestly say that I have faced death three times. You would think that the first experience would make me value my life and stop taking it for granted, but that was not the case with me. I guess at that point in time, I did not realize that I could have died, which could be why I did not take it very seriously or think about it at all. It was only after the third time that I finally started to take the blinders off; it finally hit me that I had just experienced death to the greatest extent one could possibly experience it without actually dying. If you feel like I am making little sense right now, please read on. Hopefully, things will become clearer as you get to know my story.

My First Experience with Death

In 2006, my grandmother came to visit from the Philippines. While she was here, she got a call from back home that my grandfather was dying and that he was trying to hold on so that he could see her before he passed away. Unfortunately, she did not manage to get back home in time. My family and I went to the Philippines for my grandfather's funeral. To be very honest, I did not know how to deal with his death because this was the first time someone who I loved and was close to passed away. I was confused with my feelings and almost felt emotionless because I was not crying as much as I should be. I guess I did not know how to deal with the loss.

Over time, I did learn that many people reacted in a similar way. You will see that different people grieve in a different manner. Everyone will not necessarily resort to bawling their eyes out at the death of a loved one. It is very much possible that someone just holds back and instead withdraws. However, it did feel strange for me at that time because I thought that everyone was expected to cry when faced with the death of someone they love.

Let's go back to my story now. A couple of days after the funeral, my family and I decided to go to the beach by my grandparent's house. We started off by the huts and had to walk in the water towards the beach on the other side. I had my portable DVD player with me for some reason and was carrying it above my head so it would not get wet. I was admiring the tropical view and beautiful sunny day. All of a sudden, I felt this excruciating pain and screamed at the top of my lungs like I've never done before. I put one of my arms in the water trying to fend off whatever was around me, and I ran like hell. My family was wondering what was going on. Once I reached the shore, I noticed that I had transparent tentacles wrapped around my arms and over both of my legs. I was stung by one gigantic jellyfish or several small jellyfish.

I cannot even begin to describe the pain. The closest I can compare it to was as if someone poured burning oil all over my body. Needless to say, it was the worst pain I ever felt. My family did not know how to react. My family members were saying that someone should pee on me because they were taught that when someone gets stung by a jellyfish that they should be peed on to stop the pain. I'm sure several people reading this will also have thought of the exact same thing. Yes, I know it might sound funny right now, when you are sitting in your cozy reading corner and reading about the traumatic experience I had to go through. Just trust me when I say that it was anything but funny.

My family had also heard that rubbing vinegar and lime on my wound could help stop the pain as well. However, no one peed on me or rubbed lime juice on my wounds. The option to take me to the hospital was out of the question because I was on an island and the nearest hospital was ten hours away. I just sat there on the side of the beach, rocking back and forth, hoping that the pain would soon go away. It seemed like hours passed before the pain dissipated.

What did I do after the pain went away? I went right back into the water, which shocked and surprised my family. Most people would probably become traumatized and fearful of the water and never enter it again. I thought to myself, the pain is gone, and I am not going to stop what just happened to me from enjoying the beautiful day and the water.

When I looked at myself in the mirror when I got back from the beach, it seemed like I gained a hundred pounds. My arms, along with the rest of my body, were swollen from the belly down. I still have the scars from the burns and sting marks where the jellyfish wrapped its tentacles around me. I really should have died that day. I believe my grandfather was watching over me.

Later, while I was doing some research, I came across a number of webpages and articles that provided information on how to treat jellyfish stings. If you are reading this and want to learn from the mistakes made by me (or my family, in this case), you ought to know how to treat jellyfish stings too. The first thing you should do is get the victim out of the sea or water. If the victim has been swimming in non-tropical waters, then you can simply wash the bitten area with seawater as this can deactivate the stinging cells. However, if the victim has been stung in tropical waters (by a box jellyfish, for example), then it is advised (as my family had rightly heard) to wash the bitten area with vinegar. Do not make the mistake of using fresh water or tap water because this might even make the pain worse, as it can reactivate the stinging cells.

According to the American Red Cross and the American Heart Association, if a jellyfish bites a person, the bitten area should be washed for at least thirty seconds with vinegar. However, if you do not have any vinegar on hand, you can use a solution made from baking soda instead. This will serve the same purpose of deactivating any stinging cells. Once this has been done, the American Red Cross and the American Heart Association suggest that the bitten area should be soaked in a bucket of hot water for at least twenty minutes, and ideally for longer. If you do not have access to a supply of hot water, you can choose to cover the area with an ice pack instead.

From my own experience, I know how excruciatingly painful and uncomfortable the entire process can be. This discomfort can also be treated using an oral antihistamine, which is an anti-allergy pill. A mild form of hydrocortisone cream can also be applied to the bitten area. This will help in reducing the swelling and itching that usually follows a jellyfish sting. Had my family knew to provide me with such creams and medicines, I might not have looked like the swollen monster I did when I got back home after the day at the beach.

I found an article that also talks about a similar experience.

By all accounts, ten-year-old Australian girl Rachael Shardlow should be dead. One of the world's most poisonous creatures, a box jellyfish, stung Shardlow in Australia in December, as reported by the Australian Broadcasting Corporation. After being pulled from the water with tentacles still wrapped around her legs, she amazingly lived through the attack. Her survival has baffled doctors and marine biologists, as even a miniscule amount of jellyfish venom can cause the heart to seize up and stop.

While no official tallies exist, anecdotal evidence suggests dozens of people and perhaps more than 100 or more die each year from the many species of box jellyfish that exist in all oceans.

Some 20 to 40 people die from stings by box jellyfish annually in the Philippines alone, according to the U.S. National Science Foundation. "Because death certificates are not required in many countries within the range of box jellyfish, worldwide fatalities from box jellyfish may be seriously underestimated," the NSF states.

Box jellyfish, a class that includes 50 described species, have tentacles covered in tiny biological booby traps known as cnidocysts. Each cnidocyst contains a tiny dart and a load of poison that can cause "the most explosive envenomation process that is presently known to humans," according to a 1988 paper in *The Medical Journal of Australia*.

Once the dart pierces the skin, the cnidocyst shoots the toxin through the needle and into the victim. The toxin then enters the blood, where it can cause a dangerous spike in blood pressure, stop the heart, and kill the victim, a team from Monash University in Melbourne, Australia, wrote in a 2005 paper in the journal *Toxicology Letters*.

Unlike other jellyfish, box jellyfish are agile swimmers, a skill that scientists say possibly arose because one set of their 24 eyes detects objects that get in their way.

Larger jellyfish are generally more dangerous than smaller ones because they harbor more cnidocysts. However, all jellyfish contain some poison; in fact, the phylum that all jellyfish belong to, Cnidaria, is named after their poison-producing structures.

Looking back at this near-death experience, I would say that I did take life for granted because I did not value its importance and its pricelessness. This may also have been because I did not know just how dangerous a jellyfish sting could be. It hurt, of course, but it is like looking at the bruises left from playing your favorite sport; you didn't even know they would hurt after the game. Or like realizing you went bankrupt after investing too long in all the wrong places.

What I am proud of is that I still continued to live and jumped back into the water knowing full well that I could have been stung again. A lot of people would say that this was a great deal of stupidity on my part. Instead, I believe I didn't let the fear of, "what if" stop me.

CAROL BANAYOS

My Second Experience with Death

It's February 2007, and I have just completed my second degree. During that week, I noticed that my university had a career fair. Like most other students, I thought that this was a big opportunity for me so I went ahead and I submitted my resume and a couple of days later I got a call for an interview. As luck would have it, I got the job that I started at the end of the very same month on February 26, 2007.

Eight days into the job I had to travel to Brandon, Manitoba, with my co-workers to attend a career fair. It was exciting for me because I just recently attended a career fair as a jobseeker and now as an exhibitor advertising jobs on behalf of the Province. I was quite content and satisfied at the idea of knowing that it had only been a couple of weeks since I had switched roles. If there are any fresh graduates reading this book who were lucky enough to be employed within a few days of their graduation, they will understand how big of a deal this can be at that time.

On the way home, at a stoplight, my co-workers and I were admiring the new developments. All of a sudden, a van going sixty miles an hour hits us from behind and pushes the car right through the intersection. It all happened so fast; I was sitting in the back and my co-worker and I were not wearing any seatbelts. I remember being pulled out of the window because our doors were crushed. We were all placed on a wooden stretcher and neck braces. All of us had to be rushed to the hospital and were on the wooden stretcher for several hours. They had these machines circling our bodies to determine any internal injuries or broken bones. Once the doctors had completed their assessment, they were surprised that we only had minor injuries like sprains, whiplashes and horrible headaches. It was truly a miracle. We were released and had to get a rental car to retrieve our items from the car. On the way to the car compound, we somehow ended up in a ditch and had to get towed out. It seems like luck definitely was not on our side that day because how many hindrances, obstacles and accidents is one likely to face within the span of several hours?

It felt like a series of unfortunate events occurring one after the other. We finally arrived at the car compound. I was shocked because the whole trunk was smashed in, and I just could not understand how my co-workers and I had survived; we should have been crushed. I believe my guardian angel saved my co-workers and I.

It took us approximately eighteen hours to get home to Winnipeg that day. Looking at the clock, it was about three in the morning and there was no chance that I was able to get any sleep before going in to work at eight in the morning. I had such an excruciating headache and my lower back was painfully aching, so I just laid there and went over what happened. Since it was just my second week at this new job; I didn't want to miss any work so I decided to go into work. Once my employer found out what happened, they were surprised that I came into work at all. I was sent home right away and had to go see a physiotherapist for several months to deal with my lumbar sprain and pills for my headaches. For a while after that accident, I always had a fear that someone would smash into me whenever a car pulled up close behind me. Luckily, that fear eventually went away.

Looking back at this second near-death experience, I would say that I think I was happy I survived. It's crazy because most people don't even get a first chance at life, and here I was with a second chance without really valuing my existence to the extent that I should.

This second near-death experience should have been my wake the fuck up call. I should have adopted an attitude or perspective of not taking life for granted, but that didn't happen. It was just something that happened and I got over it quickly. I never saw it as a second chance at all and it didn't make me see life differently. I didn't even begin to cherish it properly, and that's pretty sad.

If you are reading this, you must be thinking that was pretty stupid on my part. Having been through a lot in life and after having had the opportunity to reflect on what I have experienced, I would completely agree with you. If this was not a wake-up call, what was? What was going to lure me from my perpetual state of stupor? What did I need to do to really feel something? How many more times did I need fate or luck or whatever you want to call it to prod me with a stick to wake me up and make me aware of who I was and what my life was like?

CAROL BANAYOS

My Third Experience with Death

On November 11, 2009, I was crying throughout the night as I lay beside my ex-fiancé for the last time. The day prior we had decided to call it quits. I asked him to leave the house for a couple of hours while I took in this new reality. I packed all his shit by the door to expedite his departure out of my life. A month and half later, I felt a pain in my heart, and it was longing for my ex-fiancé. I felt alone and was so used to the comfort of having him around. I realized that throughout the years I had built up walls and never expressed my true feelings. I decided that I would put my pride aside and ask him to come back to me. I didn't care what the outcome was because I didn't want to have any regrets; you know how they say that it is better to have a bad experience than to live with the regret of knowing that you never tried at all.

I called him, told him that I loved him and wanted to work things out and that we shouldn't throw away what we had. Unfortunately for me, we were not on the same page; he did not want to work things out or get back together. I told him that I respected his decision and wished him the best in life and love. Little did I know, he already had moved on and cheated on me while we were together and got his new chick pregnant. The funny thing is that two months prior to us breaking up, I had a conversation with my sister-in-law, and I told her that I wished he would just cheat on me and leave. Wow, talk about, "Ask and you shall receive." Learn a small lesson from this too, readers. Be careful what you wish for because you might just get it all. As you skim through the pages of this book, it is important that you let this one percent of it sink in to the back of your mind. Be very careful of what you desire to attain in life because it may either be the reason for your pain or the cause behind your of happiness.

It turns out that he regretted us breaking up; he said he always wanted to marry me and have kids together. What is also somewhat hilarious is that my friend lent me a book to read several months back and just left it on my work desk under my paperwork. I looked at the book and the title was, "How to be Single." I later laughed my ass off at the irony. It was a great book and it really helped me to get over the breakup. I realized that this was the first time I was single in over ten years and was excited to get to know myself again. I could now get into all those activities that he was not interested in participating in. I could go to all those places that he did not want to visit. I could order in my favorite food that I had not been able to have for so long because he did not really like it. I could give myself all the time that I needed to pamper myself. I could spend all the time I wanted to with my family and girlfriends without having anyone complain that I was not giving them enough attention, no complaints about my supposedly selfish behavior. Now was the time when I could explore everything that I had always wanted to in order to satiate my curious nature and indulge in all the luxuries I had secretly dreamed of indulging myself in.

Looking back at the situation, I realized that my gut was telling me all along that this relationship was not right. Maybe I really should have listened to this feeling. However, like most people, I found it hard to accept what my instincts were telling me. The thought of being alone was scary and daunting and it just seemed so comfortable to have someone around. There is another small lesson here for you, readers. What I forgot was that being with someone is just not enough. You need to be with the *right* person. Your definition of the right person may be very different from mine, but a basic description would be that even their imperfections are acceptable to you, with or without compromise. It is better to accept the person as a whole, rather than cherry picking on parts of theirs being your favorite. They say that the reason that brings you together can be the cause of your separation. So, choose wisely who you decide to keep by your side through life's journey. This should be done carefully and with caution.

At that point in life, I just thought it was right to progress with the relationship and finally say yes to his proposal. I was too weak to leave the relationship and call it quits because I already broke up with him two times before and had always taken him back. I felt that if I were to break up again, it would end up the same way. He would apologize to me or I would miss him and then we would end up back together. I was quite miserable in the relationship and, although I feel a little sad and ashamed to admit this, I lost myself. I isolated myself from my friends and family and never wanted to go out. I looked at myself in the mirror, not recognizing the person staring back at me. I was in pain and felt depressed. I turned towards food to numb and overcome the feeling of pain and emptiness that came with the depression.

I would fill myself up with ginormous meals and could not stop myself from consuming excessive amounts of food. Not surprisingly, I was the biggest I have ever been, which was very difficult for me to accept as I had thought I would never gain weight because I was always fit and athletic. It got so bad that I contemplated committing suicide on many occasions because my irrational fucked up mind convinced myself that this was an easier way out. Again, it was only later that I realized that I was not the only one who felt this way. Having altered eating habits are a very common sign of depression and many people have reported that they either ate too much or ate nothing at all during their condition. Similarly, it is also not uncommon for someone in a position like mine to feel suicidal. Yes, everyone does not feel this way, but there are people out there (and I am assuming that a handful of you people who are reading this are also included in this) who have felt this way. This is no sign of being weak or being vulnerable.

It is simply an indicator that one needs to change something in his or her life.

Prior to this relationship, I broke up with my first love, which was a very traumatic experience in itself. He was my "everything," but I could not stand the lies and cheating. Because of these issues in particular, I developed a lot of insecurities. I blamed myself like it was all my fault; had he lied and cheated on me because I wasn't good enough for him? This basically meant that I was at an all-time low; there was a severe lack of self-esteem, lack of self-confidence, and my self-worth was non-existent. I did not give myself enough time to heal before I got together with my ex-fiancé and, therefore, I was truly not emotionally available for him or anyone else. Therein lies the start of a relationship with a weak foundation. However, I do realize that I have to hold myself accountable and take responsibility for how these relationships ended. I was just as much part of the problem because I was not true to myself and ignored my intuition.

I was with my ex-fiancé for seven long years: 2002 to 2009. During those years, I had three near-death experiences. I never appreciated the many chances that I was given to start the beautiful gift of life all over again because I was already dead inside, nothing more than an empty shell. As painful as the break up was, I felt a sense of relief; it was as if a heavy weight had been lifted off my shoulders. I felt much lighter and freer from any pressure or tension. I truly believe now that it was a blessing in disguise. I thank God and my guardian angels for watching over me by letting the relationship end before I ended myself. Because this could have happened if the relationship had not ended. With the death of this relationship and my old self comes a rebirth that allowed me a fourth chance at life.

I learned a lot from this relationship, which resulted in my rebirth. I learned that you have to allow yourself to heal before you enter a new relationship and that you should always follow your gut. Give yourself all the time you need, it is never too little or too much. Some people might bounce back very quickly after a break up or any other setback in life, whereas others need more time to come to terms with what has happened and to slowly secure their own footing again. Another thing I learned was that compatibility in regards to ambitions, values and characteristics are very important when getting into a relationship. If you hold completely different values from your significant other, then chances are that you might not work out in the long run. For example, if you find your other half making comments about how they believe it is okay to have a little fun outside of the relationship, it means that loyalty and fidelity are not values that they hold very close to their heart. If you are in complete agreement then congratulations, you two were lucky enough to end up together. However, if you try to brush it off or laugh it off and agree with them only to avoid making them unhappy or losing them, let me warn you that you have lost them already. This is because, sooner or later, they will act on their words and leave you standing in a position where you can't even ask them how they could put you in this state. At that point, willingly or unwillingly, you will have to let go of your partner.

In addition, I learned that you should not want to get into a relationship to make you "whole." You do not need "another half" because you are already whole. Both people in the relationship should be whole and have the ability to enhance their own lives. You should be able to function and live on your own and your partner should be there to enhance the positive aspects of life for you. You should never put your self-worth, happiness or personal well-being at stake, or be dependent on a partner because this would make your life very unstable and volatile. I learned never to settle, I learned how to value my self-worth, and I learned how to be brave enough to call it quits in relationships that do not serve me. I learned to say no to people whom I had toxic relationships with. Most importantly, this personal rebirth allowed me to realize and accept the fact that my old self had to die in order for this new outlook to unfold and blossom. As they say, 'the phoenix must burn to emerge.'

CHAPTER 1 – EXERCISE

Check out www.carolbanayos.com/bonuses to complete the Chapter 1 Exercise for Near-Death Experience and Rebirth.

CHAPTER 2

Conscious Awareness

"Awareness is a great agent for change."
Eckhart Tolle

The second book that I stumbled upon after my break up with my ex-fiancé was "A New Earth: Awakening to Your Life's Purpose" by Eckhart Tolle. After reading this book, I realized that during my near-death experiences, I was asleep, an empty lifeless vessel stuck in mundane daily tasks and operating like a robot. I was nothing more than a zombie walking around aimlessly, unaware of myself and completely oblivious to the world around me. I knew that if I didn't regard my third near-death experience as I did then I would still be a zombie, an empty vessel asleep at the wheel of life. I started to think to myself about how many people operated their lives like this and how it was important for people, for the entire world, to wake the fuck up from their sleep. It is important to become awakened and consciously aware.

You may ask, isn't being conscious and being aware the same thing? No, it's not. People can be conscious but not be *aware* of their consciousness. So what really is the difference between being aware and being conscious? I think it is important for us to look at them both separately and try to understand that before we begin to move forward.

Let's look at an example. If you find yourself in the middle of a steep hiking path with a bear coming down from one end, chances are that you are going to run in order to save your life. As you run, hike or scramble across the trail, you hear the thumping of the bear behind you, which gives you an adrenaline rush. You look around here and there, trying to find a way to escape. At this point, you will be very aware of all that is around you: trees, animals, rocks, sand, everything. You will, of course, also be aware of the animal that is running after you. At the same time, however, you will also be conscious of the fact that your life is at risk and that it is also possible that your life may end sooner than what you had thought. This is called the human instinct, something all humans have instilled in them since primitive times. For instance, humans would feel an adrenaline rush whenever a potential threat or prey approach. This way, they would act immediately according to their emotional reasoning.

I hope that the example clarifies the difference between being aware and being conscious. Hopefully, you know by now that being aware and being conscious are completely different concepts, even though most people think that they have the exact same connotation.

Let's go into a little more depth to see what it means to be aware. If you find out, for example, that a heavy thunderstorm is due to occur in the evening, you know that it is going to take place. This means that you are aware that it will happen. However, even though you have this information, there is little you know about where exactly there will be a thunderstorm, how bad the storm will be, the extent to which it will cause damage to the city, and so on. In other words, you can also say that the term "being aware" has a physically related expression. For example, if you drink a lot of Coke, you will be aware that it can cause diseases like diabetes and obesity. You are aware of the fact that if you are doing well academically, your parents will be happy and that certain actions you take can hurt the people you love. You are also aware of the realities of your life due to the presence of factors such as cognitive abilities, sensations, knowledge and perception. This basically means that when you are aware of something, you do not fully know exactly how it will impact your life and to what extent your life will be influenced by one particular factor. Awareness is tied with feelings because it co-relates with emotional intelligence. You cannot possibly be consciously aware of your surroundings if you are not sensitive towards them on an emotional level. For instance, a person getting in an accident should instantly make you want to help them because you feel emotionally sensitive to their pain and are aware of their condition.

Now let's try to understand what it means for us to be conscious. To some, it might seem like being conscious means that one needs to be a little spiritual as well. This does not mean that you need to start seeing signs from whatever deity you believe in and see demons left, right and center. It means that you need to have the insight or the degree of awareness, such that the physical world does not serve as an obstruction in your understanding of what is happening within and around you. This means that one has to be fully aware and cognizant of the metaphysical realm, which is where it is believed that spiritual interactions occur and one begins to learn beyond the average individual's tangible experience. In essence, this implies that the state of being conscious goes far and beyond the state of just simply being aware.

However, in order for an individual to be conscious, he or she needs to be aware. If you are not aware of a certain event, object, place or factor, then it is not possible for you to be conscious of it. For example, in the example of the bear rumbling after you on a hiking trail, we saw that it was obvious that you were fully aware of what was going on in your surroundings and, at the same time, you were also consciously trying to find a way to escape and save your life. This basically means that for the time being, you did not focus too much on everything and narrowed it down instead to only focus on certain aspects. At times like these, it is more important to be emotionally intelligent.

A lot of people seem to have full faith in the quote, "Knowledge is power." Indeed, why shouldn't it be? I feel like that is the point where consciousness and awareness pick up from, almost like a revolution's starting point. If you have read so far and even if you are just a teenager or twenty-something, you will know that we do have a substantial amount of free will. This means that we also have the choice of being conscious and aware, or both, or neither at all. Thus, where you end up and where destiny takes you actually does rely very heavily on the kind of decisions that you make.

In some ways, the reason why so much emphasis is laid on knowledge is because it makes one aware of his or her worldly realities and, therefore, makes an individual more conscious about the fact that there is a bigger and better purpose to his or her life; there is some sort of higher calling. Although some things might seem to be completely random and out of place, always remember that there is a reason behind everything. You might simply not be fully aware of it at that time. As soon as you decide that you want to do something about it and begin to question why something happened or turned out the way it did, and as soon as you begin reasoning out the realities of life, you will find yourself becoming more conscious. Thus, now you know why knowledge is important and how knowledge is the starting point on the chain of realization.

In general, if you are able to ever achieve a state of being aware and conscious at the same time, you will find how big of an impact that can have on you and your life. For example, it is common knowledge that being more aware of yourself and the world around you will ensure that you make the better decision. However, it is only when you become conscious of the influence of various factors in your life that you are able to make the best possible decisions.

Another question that you can ask me at this point is: what really is the point? Why and how do knowledge, consciousness and awareness affect our life?

Let's start with knowledge. When you use the knowledge that you have learnt, you can actively decide on the various aspects of intervention. Once you know whether something is bad or good, you will see that you find yourself in a better position as far as making a decision is concerned about whether you should include that in your life or not. For example, if you know that consuming too much alcohol is not good for you, you can make a better decision as far as your dietary habits are concerned and simply avoid alcoholic beverages altogether or cut down on how much alcohol you consume on a daily or weekly basis. This is the point where you begin to gain awareness.

You can also use your knowledge as a base for judgment, which, in turn, allows you to discover the various options that are available to you and pursue one that suits your liking. For example, if you know that too much sugar is not good for you, you can try to come with other alternatives that are healthier to the food items you normally consume that contain a high sugar level. This can be seen as a perfect example of an individual applying his or her awareness and becoming more responsible. Now, such an individual may find himself or herself on the verge of becoming more conscious. At this point, do not be alarmed if you start to question your own knowledge.

Once you start questioning yourself, you will know that you have come closer and closer to the state of being conscious. At this stage, you will slowly be able to pull out and identify the main reason behind the various occurrences in your life. Eventually, you can join the dots together and you will feel that life suddenly starts making more sense to you. This will allow you to find out what the ultimate purpose of your life really is. At this point, you can consider yourself to be fully aware. As you become more and more aware, you will feel an increase in your vibrational frequencies. This will provide you with the protection you need against the negative factors that plague life from time to time and you will be able to see and think outside the box. Eventually, you will become more conscious of yourself, your purpose, your realities, and even the higher calling.

Therefore, being consciously aware requires you to observe the thoughts that you think about and how they affect you. For example, when you are thinking negative thoughts, you are conscious of those thoughts and then you become aware of how those negative thoughts and states affect you. By being consciously aware, you can begin to shift your thoughts to something positive. From my experience and from the stories I have heard, this shift to conscious awareness usually comes from within a person, when he or she finally awakens from a tragic event. Finally throwing in the towel because they are sick and tired of being sick and tired, it seems as if this is the moment when people begin to rise. The only way to improve and change their current circumstances is to have that realization and to make a decision that a change in them is required. As change is inevitable, the first step towards it, is to have the will and determination to make the transformation happen. Only then can anything substantial come out of it.

It is also important to point out that whatever thoughts we think will plant a seed in our subconscious. At this point, let us try to understand what the subconscious really is.

In order to understand what the subconscious is, we need to be clear about what the conscious mind is first. The conscious part of the mind is held responsible for reasoning and logic. For example, if I ask you to tell me what the sum of two plus two is, your conscious mind will be put to work while you are carrying out that addition.

In addition to this, the conscious part of the mind also controls the actions that we do intentionally. For example, if you decide to stretch your legs, which are a voluntary action, then this will be controlled by the conscious. In short, if you are aware of any action that you are carrying out, then that will be done by conscious mind. For example, if you are given a cup of tea and you decide to take a sip that is the doing of the conscious mind.

Some people also refer to the conscious mind as being the gatekeeper of the mind. If you read a statement somewhere that does not fit into the belief system you adhere to, for example, then the conscious mind will filter it out. The same thing happens when you are called names or criticized. For instance, if someone has low self-esteem or self-worth they may believe they are stupid. So should caution that If I tell you that you are dumb, your conscious mind will filter it out and let you know that you are not actually dumb.

Now, let's come to the subconscious mind. The subconscious mind is that part that is held responsible for all the involuntary actions you carry out. For example, have you ever paused to think that hey, I need to make my heart beat a little faster right now or I need to blink a little more to keep out all the dust from my eyes? No, you will never find yourself consciously thinking about these things.

In most cases, when we are breathing, our subconscious mind is taking control of it. If, however, you intentionally hold your breath sometimes (if you are under water, for example), then your conscious mind has taken over for the time being. The subconscious mind can basically be seen as the storage space for everything that is not being controlled by or held in your conscious mind. This includes your beliefs, previous life experiences, skills, memories and emotions. Sometimes you may be feeling certain emotions (such as anger, guilt or sorrow) that you do not intentionally want to feel but at the same time there is nothing that you can do about them. Those emotions are being regulated by your subconscious mind at that time.

Let's look at an example to understand the exact difference between the conscious and unconscious mind, because it may appear to be a very fluid concept for some people. Think back to the time when you were first learning how to drive a car. In the beginning, you probably paid a lot of attention to where you were going and which gear you needed to change into (if you had a manual car) and so on. If someone spoke to you while you were driving, you probably asked him or her to shut up and let you focus. At this time, you were using your conscious mind while driving.

However, after practicing for a couple of weeks, you were probably able to feel more in control. You didn't consciously have to think about switching gears or speeding up or hitting the brake. Although listening to loud music or carrying conversations with another passenger does not put you at risk while driving, texting is not advisable as it puts your life in danger. This is because this skill that you were learning transferred from the conscious mind to the subconscious mind. Your conscious mind was now free to focus on other things.

Our subconscious is the part of the mind of which one is not fully aware, but which influences one's actions and feelings. So if we plant negative seeds we will bear the bitter fruits. Similarly, if we plant positive seeds we bear the sweetness.

Our brains tend to work on different thought patterns. You can almost compare it to the way you program your computers and other electronic devices. In some cases, you will be able to identify a certain pattern within the thoughts that are produced by your brain.

When you plant negative seeds in your brain, you bear the bitter fruits because all your thought processes have an underlying negative tone. Everything you see or hear or come across is interpreted in a negative manner. This becomes problematic because you are often unable to figure out the root cause of these negative thoughts.

Instead, you end up believing them and letting them define you and your experiences.

What you need to realize is that these thought patterns are actually constructed by you yourself. It was you who initially sowed the seeds of negativity. These thought patterns simply came into existence because you thought those thoughts so many times and so frequently that they became ingrained into your subconscious as an automatic way of thinking and functioning.

Eckhart Tolle states, "Awakening is a shift in consciousness in which thinking and awareness separate. For most people it is not an event but a process they undergo. Even those rare beings who experience a sudden, dramatic, and seemingly irreversible awakening will still go through a process in which the new state of consciousness gradually flows into and transforms everything they do and so becomes integrated into their lives. Instead of being lost in your thinking, when you are awake you recognize yourself as the awareness behind it. Thinking then ceases to be a self-serving autonomous activity that takes possession of you and runs your life. Awareness takes over from thinking. Instead of being in charge of your life, thinking becomes the servant of awareness. Awareness is conscious connection with universal intelligence. Another word for it is presence; consciousness without thought."

The words of Tolle Eckhart resonate with me and it is due to this very reason that they had such a profound impact on me, and my life. After reading the book, I began to feel that things in my life started to change and I am happy to say that I was also ready for it. You know how that saying goes: when the student is ready, the teacher will appear. Well, this student right here was ready and you can say that this was the start of an amazing journey.

My mentor shared a poem with me that was written by Sonny Carroll. It brought me to a river of tears because it mirrored what I had gone through to get to my awakening or, as I like to call it, my wake-the-fuck-up call.

A time comes in your life when you finally get it...

When in the midst of all your fears and insanity you stop dead in your tracks and somewhere, the voice inside you cries out ENOUGH! Enough fighting and crying or struggling to hold on. And, like a child quieting down after a blind tantrum... Your sobs begin to subside, you shudder once or twice, you blink back your tears and through a mantle of wet lashes you begin to look at the world through new eyes.

This is your awakening...

You realize that it's time to stop hoping and waiting for something to change or for happiness, safety and security to come galloping over the next horizon. You come to terms with the fact that he/she is not Prince Charming or Snow White. That in the real world, there aren't always fairytale endings (or beginnings for that matter) and that any guarantee of "happily ever after" must begin with you. In the process, a sense of serenity is born of acceptance. You awaken to the fact that you are not perfect and that not everyone will always love, appreciate or approve of who or what you are, and that's okay. You learn the importance of loving and championing yourself and in the process a sense of newfound confidence is born of self-approval. You stop complaining and blaming other people for the things they did to you, and you learn that the only thing you can count on is the unexpected. You learn that people don't always say what they mean or mean what they say and that not everyone will always be there for you and that it's not always about you.

So, you learn to stand on your own and to take care of yourself and in the process a sense of safety and security is born of self-reliance. You stop judging and pointing fingers, and you begin to accept people as they are and overlook their shortcomings and human frailties, and in the process a sense of peace and contentment is born of forgiveness. You realize that much of the way you view yourself, and the world around you is as a result of all the messages and opinions that have been ingrained into your psyche. You begin to sift through all the stuff you've been fed, about how you should behave, how you should look and how much you should weigh, what you should wear and where you should shop and what you should drive, how and where you should live and what you should do for a living, who you should marry and what you should expect of a relationship, the importance of having and raising children or what you owe your parents. You learn to open up to new worlds and different points of view, and you begin reassessing and redefining who you are, what you really stand for. You learn the difference between wanting and needing, and you begin to discard the doctrines and values you've outgrown, or should never have bought into to begin with and in the process you learn to go with your instincts.

You learn that it is truly in giving that we receive and that there is power and glory in creating and contributing, and you stop maneuvering through life merely as a "consumer". You learn that principles such as honesty and integrity are not the outdated ideals of a bygone era but the mortar that holds together the foundation upon which you must build a life. You learn that you don't know everything, it's not your job to save the world. You learn to distinguish between guilt and responsibility and the importance of setting boundaries. You learn that the only cross to bear is the one you choose to carry.

Then you learn about love. Romantic love and familial love. How to love, how much to give in love, when to stop giving and when to walk away. You learn not to project your needs or your feelings onto a relationship. You learn that you will not be more beautiful, more intelligent, more loveable or important because of the man or woman on your arm or the child that bears your name. You learn to look at relationships as they really are and not as you would have them be. You stop trying to control people, situations and outcomes. You learn that just as people grow and change so it is with love, and you learn that you don't have the right to demand love on your terms. You learn that alone does not mean lonely... You look in the mirror and come to terms with the fact that you will never be a size five or a perfect ten and you stop trying to compete with the image inside your head and agonizing over how you "stack up.

You also stop working so hard at putting your feelings aside, smoothing things over and ignoring your needs. You learn that feelings of entitlement are perfectly okay and that it is your right to want things and to ask for the things that you want... and that sometimes it is necessary to make demands. You come to the realization that you deserve to be treated with love, kindness, sensitivity and respect, and you won't settle for less. And, you allow only the hands of a lover who cherishes you to glorify you with their touch and in the process you internalize the meaning of self-respect. You learn that your body really is your temple and you begin to care for it and treat it with respect. You begin eating a balanced diet, drinking more water and taking more time to exercise. You learn that fatigue diminishes the spirit and can create doubt and fear. So you take more time to rest. And, just as food fuels the body, laughter fuels our soul. So you take more time to laugh and to play. You learn that anything worth achieving is worth working for and that wishing for something to happen is different from working toward making it happen. More importantly, you learn that in order to achieve you need direction, discipline, and perseverance. You also learn that no one can do it all alone and that it's OK to risk asking for help.

You learn that the only thing you must truly fear is ... FEAR itself. You learn to step right into and through your fears because you know that whatever happens you can handle it and to give in to fear is to give away the right to live life on your terms. You learn that life isn't always fair, you don't always get what you think you deserve and that sometimes bad things happen to unsuspecting, good people. On these occasions you learn not to personalize things, it's just life happening. You learn to deal with the ego. You learn that negative feelings such as anger, envy and resentment must be understood and redirected, or they will suffocate the life out of you and poison the universe that surrounds you. You learn to admit when you are wrong and to building bridges instead of walls. You learn to be thankful and to take comfort in many of the simple things we take for granted, things that millions of people upon the earth can only dream about: a full refrigerator, clean running water, a soft warm bed, a long hot shower. Slowly, you begin to take responsibility for yourself by yourself, and you make a promise to not betray yourself and to settle for less than your heart's desire. You hang a wind chime outside your

CAROL BANAYOS

window so you can listen to the wind. And you make it a point to keep smiling, to keep trusting, and to stay open to every wonderful possibility.

Finally, with courage and conviction in your heart and soul you take a stand, you take a deep breath and begin to design the life you want to live... .as best as you can.

CHAPTER 2 – EXERCISE

Check out www.carolbanayos.com/bonuses to complete the Chapter 2 Exercise for Conscious Awareness.

CHAPTER 3

Spirituality

"You have no need to travel anywhere. Journey within yourself, enter a mine of rubies and bathe in the splendor of your own light." Rumi

What is spirituality?

"A broad, inclusive definition is: spirituality is that which gives meaning to one's life and draws one to transcend oneself. Spirituality is a broader concept than religion, although that is one expression of spirituality. Other expressions include prayer, meditation, interactions with others or nature, and relationship with God or a higher power."

In the spring of 2010, I went to a group meditation that included the use of Tibetan singing bowls. We were all told to lay down on our yoga mats with our eyes closed. If we had some energy blockages, the instructor would come around and work on us. It was at this time that I felt an energy and presence hovering over me. The instructor was working on my blockages in my head, throat, and belly area. All of a sudden, I hear a loud ring. The Tibetan bowl was right by my head, and I was freaking out because as the ringing was taken place I saw the sound vibrations. It was a beautiful rainbow of colors that rippled out on the left and right side. My mind then went completely blank and all I could see was pitch-black darkness with no images at all. As soon as the instructor would say something, an image would appear. For example, she said "heart" and all I saw was a red heart while the background remained black.

I left that class thinking I had gone bat shit crazy, seeing all these sounds, vibrations, and blankness. I kept that experience to myself for several months and did not mention it to anybody at all. However, I ended up telling my co-worker, who was also my mentor at the time. He convinced me that I should call her in order to find out what happened to me. I gathered my courage and called her. I told her my experience, and she said that I had a spiritual awakening. My third eye was now open. She also mentioned that most people do not get to experience what I did in their entire lifetime, and that I should feel blessed and grateful. I was, indeed, very grateful for what I was able to experience. I had never heard anyone else talk about a similar experience through the practice of yoga, meditation, or any other stress-relieving exercise. Another reason why I thought that this experience meant, that I was going mad. After speaking to her, I was relieved that I was not going crazy and decided to embrace the start of this new spiritual journey.

I would term this experience as being very essential for my mental wellbeing and purification. There are a number of different things that one can do to achieve this state of wellbeing through meditation, some of which are focused on yoga, while others are based on compassion, transcendentalism and mindfulness. Regardless of the kind of technique you choose, they will most likely bring about the same effect, given that they have been carried out properly.

There are several advantages and benefits that one can gain from meditation. One thing that meditating allows us to do is relieve stress, which is an essential part that needs to be achieved when one begins undertaking this spiritual journey. With the problems faced by an individual in their everyday life, it is not surprising that stress levels are soaring and that there is a sharp increase in the use of anti-anxiety medication to curb the increase in agitation that these individuals are undergoing. However, with meditation, I can personally tell you that it makes you feel that you are in charge of your own emotions and nervous system. In fact, several studies have also been done on this very subject and the results of most studies reported that people found it easier to regulate their own emotions after they had meditated. Thus, you feel more empowered. A lot of people also report feeling an improvement in their levels of concentration as a result of meditation. There are fewer chances of them being distracted. Several related studies also concluded that some people have been able to multitask much better thanks to meditation because they remain focused on what needs to be done and by what time instead of getting phased out if a number of different tasks have to be managed at the same time. Many people who are involved in some sort of meditation believe that taking out some time to meditate helps you to get in touch with your inner source of energy, which results in an improvement in focus and memory.

Meditation is also a well-known practice for increasing one's self-awareness. It is often suggested to individuals who feel that they blow up on very small issues and react very strongly to very minor or insignificant events. For example, a person may lash out very violently if something slightly annoying takes place in his or her life. However, meditation serves the purpose of making such individuals more aware of the problem with their reaction or behavior. Once an individual becomes more aware of his or her anger, it becomes easier to detach the self from it. This helps in calming down the person and clearing their mind. Once a person becomes more aware of themselves, they also lose the need to put up a façade in front of others and will begin becoming comfortable in their own skin.

Not only does it increase self-awareness, but meditation also helps a person come to terms with the self. This means that a person becomes more accepting of who he or she is as a person, of both their positive and negative traits and how these impact their life. People have been known to say that their life has completely changed because of meditation. Although, external factors have remained as they are, individuals are able to cope with them better and remain happy and content with what they have. As has been discussed in one of the chapters in this book, this means that meditation helps a person to become more aware and more conscious. One always needs to be consciously aware in order to ever dream of personal growth and development.

At the start of my journey, I often felt repressed, restrained and bogged down. I spent a lot of time being unhappy with myself and with my life. It was only slowly and gradually that I was able to pull out of this depressive phase. A study was carried out at Johns Hopkins to study the link between meditation (more specifically, mindfulness meditation) and symptoms of pain, depression and anxiety. The results of the scientific study indicated that meditation plays a big role in training the brain to reduce symptoms of anxiety, pain and damage. At this point, let me remind you that I am not promising you or providing you with any guarantee that it will automatically cure you of any negative thoughts that are triggering your depression. However, it is a very effective way of managing the symptoms of depression, which means that it leaves a person feeling more content.

There are numerous ways in which you can try to incorporate meditation into your everyday life. You do not even need to give it a lot of time. Even fifteen minutes should be more than enough for some people. Before starting, try to make your body relax physically while stretching a little and making sure that your posture is correct. You can sit in a lotus position, but if that is too difficult, you can simply sit on a chair. Furthermore, you can also relax your abdomen and breathe from the diaphragm. This is a good time to remember God, to remember the souls of people who hold a truly inspirational role in your life, and to think about one's own higher inner self. Simple breathing exercises can make for very good meditation and allow the body to relax and the mind to focus. Try to take a deep breath in and count to ten or twelve. The simple routine you need to follow should be all about inhaling, retaining and then exhaling. Once you begin to consciously relax the different parts of your body, you will become aware of just how tense your body usually is. Relax your feet, your legs, your hips, your abdomen, your arms, your hands, your shoulders, your face and, of course, your brain.

If this routine does not make you feel at ease at first, you can repeat it a couple of times until you begin to feel more relaxed. It is possible that it may take you even a couple of days or more before you can get into the routine perfectly but, as they say, practice does make perfect. While you are meditating, try to focus on the present: on the here and the now. Let go of all your thoughts about the future and all the memories of the past. If, however, a thought does threaten to cross your mind, let it. Do not consciously try to push it out of your mind because you will, once again, become focused on something other than relaxing.

Visualization exercises can also help some people. Many experts offer recorded videos and audio-cassettes that you can listen to and follow in order to carry out visualization. These programs usually give out detailed instructions, such as what to imagine or what to do at each point.

Yoga has also been gaining increasing popularity in recent years across the world, such as Moksha yoga and Bikram yoga. They are both different forms of hot yoga, which is carried out at a very high temperature. Bikram yoga is considered to be the original form of hot yoga. Classes of Bikram yoga focus largely on 26 different postures and lay great emphasis on endurance. Moksha yoga, on the other hand, was the brainchild of two yogis based in Toronto. The motivation behind this form of yoga was that these people wanted to incorporate an environmental aspect into their hot yoga routine. For example, they tried to be more green through having things like sustainable flooring and energy-efficient heating. Although there is a heavy debate currently going on with regards to whether hot yoga is actually beneficial or not, many yoga directors claim that hot yoga, such as Bikram yoga (which I have also tried out for myself and I really enjoy and love it), actually help in improving one's breathing and also allows one to develop better mental focus. This helps to improve concentration.

With greater mental clarity, you will be able to look at yourself, at your problems, and the world around from another perspective, which may end up being your key to the path of personal growth and development. Regardless of the kind of yoga that you wish to engage in, I am sure you all will agree that it feels incredibly empowering to know that you are in charge of your body, your health and your emotions. It helps you become more aware of the fact that there is an internal locus of control, not an external one.

"Spiritual awakening is a kind of flowering of consciousness. When consciousness expands and opens into a new expression, we call that a spiritual awakening. And while there are as many kinds of awakenings as there are flowers, they are all equally mysterious. What is it that causes a child to start to awaken to the nature of words and language? What causes the awakening of sexuality in a teenager? How does one suddenly know they are falling in love? Or even more profoundly, how does one explain the birth of unconditional or divine love? Finally, what are the causes of the most profound spiritual awakenings, where consciousness suddenly recognizes its ultimate true nature? Why does that type of flowering appear in one consciousness today and another one tomorrow? If the formula for a simple petunia is a vastly complex interplay of earthly, human, and even cosmic forces, then imagine how complex the formula is for the unfolding of a human consciousness into full spiritual enlightenment as one's true nature. The good news is that we cannot and do not need to know the totality of the formula involved to grow some petunias, and we cannot and do not need to know the formula for spiritual enlightenment. Yet, we can be curious about all of the factors involved and even play with them to see what effects, if any, they may have in our individual experience of consciousness unfolding."

The journey to spirituality made me realize that we are not physical beings having a spiritual experience. We are spiritual beings having a human/physical experience here on earth. This realization made me remember my roots and strengthen my belief on who I was this whole time. By knowing this truth, we awaken our spirituality and a choice is made to discover our own true sense of being, whatever that may mean to you on a personal level. With that choice you realize that what you always needed was within you this whole time. This journey has made me realize that we spend most of our small, finite life seeking out things that are outside our reach and things that we perceive we are not worthy of. We feel that that those things will complete the void within us and make us feel whole. We feel that those things will be the vessel through which we can become the person we have always wanted to be. We feel that achieving or obtaining this thing will be the key to a greater life ahead. However, this is where we are wrong, or at least where I was wrong. We often do not need any external object, human or event to make us into who we want to be and get us where we are destined too. It is all within *us*. You are wrong if you reckon joy emanates principally from human relationships.

I do believe in a higher power and choose to call that higher power God. This power lies in everything and anything we might experience. We just have to have the courage to turn against habitual lifestyles and engage in unconventional living for a while. Please don't think that I am trying to enforce my belief on you. You can call your god by any name or believe in any deity. However, for me, it was and always remains God. At my times of great darkness, when I felt as if I was hurtling down a bottomless well, God brought me to the light. You don't know that God is all you have, when God is all you got.

My belief in a higher power has brought me this sense of oneness. This oneness does not just extend to God; it extends to the universe and earth and all that it inhabits and encompasses. I feel the oneness the most when I am out in nature, engulfed by the trees and its mirrored reflection in the water while soaking in the sunshine and ravishing in the beauty and the serenity. I feel this oneness when I stop for a second in the middle of a long commute from one end of the city to another and hear the soft, soothing chirping of birds. I feel this oneness when I feel the breeze rippling through my hair and I feel this oneness when I feel the rain washing away my sorrows, my grief, my weaknesses, my flaws, and making me pure, whole and clean once more.

This feeling of oneness with everything also brings out and increases your level of kindness, compassion and love. I feel blessed because I have been lucky enough to arrive at the stage where I am today. This current position in life offers me the vantage point through which I can view life, which allows me to see life through my love glasses. I am at a point in life where I feel that my happiness comes from within me; it is no longer contingent upon what others say, what others do or what kind of material gains that life has to offer me. Happiness cannot be sought after through external sources, but is something one creates within their own selves. Happiness born from within forms the true essence of peace and bliss needed to be comfortable in your own skin. I am not saying there are no setbacks, no hurdles, no obstacles, no hindrances, no sorrows. There *is* negativity. Simply saying that there is nothing bad in the world and denying the very existence of negativity when it is staring you in the face would only reflect my lack of knowledge, nothing more. Therefore, I would advise you all to accept it as well. Still, what I have come to realize is that this negativity is also balanced out by positivity, like the Chinese concept of yin and yang. As they say: it is always darkest before the dawn. This means that everyone does pass through trying times during which they may feel small, little and meaningless, but those times come and go. One must not lose his or her vision or focus during these trying times; you should be even more resolute in your efforts to move past this crucial stage.

CHAPTER 3 – EXERCISE

Check out www.carolbanayos.com/bonuses to complete the Chapter 3 Exercise for Spirituality.

CHAPTER 4

Personal Growth and Development

"The greatest gift you can give to somebody is your own personal development.

I used to say, 'If you will take care of me, I will take care of you.'

Now I say, 'I will take care of me for you, if you will take of you for me.'" Jim Rohn

Waking the fuck up and having this new sense of conscious awareness awakened my hunger to improve and strengthen all facets of my being, with my ultimate goal being to grow more as a person. I did feel alone because I did not meet anyone else who had the same outlook as me in life. I felt bad and strange about my desire of reaching new heights, so I kept things to myself.

Now that I think back to it, I probably did not need to feel bad about it. Why should I? Every individual in this world has set out on their own path and every person aspires to achieve something different. This is because most of us, if not all, have a unique perspective from which we view life. Some of us are focused only on material gain, some of us are focused on feeding our inner souls and propelling ourselves towards growth, development and change, while there are others who fall somewhere in between. What I am trying to say is this: if we all start thinking about it and come up with the idea that not having the same view, perspective or goal as others makes us weird, then we are all very, very weird. Should that be a bad thing? Not at all. Is it bad that we do not share the perspective of a cold-blooded murderer who kills innocent women and children for his own interest or gain? I don't think so. Then why should any other difference in perspectives make us feel weird or unhappy with ourselves? There you go, some more advice for readers.

Even if the rest of this book goes over your head and there is nothing you can gain from it at all, then do remember one thing. There is nothing wrong about viewing the world though someone else's perspective. I mean, if I were to think that my book was the best thing that ever happened to the world or you thought it was nothing more than a confused soul venting out in a diary, then so be it. I have my own perspective and you have yours. We might agree on certain views and disagree on others, which is perfectly fine. Yet, at the same time, it is very important to respect each other's point on view as well.

My personal development began approximately six years ago. I went to visit my sister-in-law in Vancouver and she told me I should take this personal development course with her through this company. I was a bit hesitant at first and replied by saying, "If I am going to take a personal development course, I will take it with someone who is one of the best in the world." So I obviously did not end up taking that course. I do not know whether that was a smart thing to say or do. Maybe it was, or maybe it just reflected my own ignorance. Either way, I left Vancouver without taking the course. I went back home to Winnipeg, woke up one morning and was staring right at Tony Robbins.

At this point, you may be wondering what importance Tony Robbins holds in my life. Back in 2009, I made a vision board and on this vision board, I put people on there who I admired, looked up to and respected. Why was it important for me to create a vision board? Well, there are a number of reasons. A vision board helps you to create what you would ideally want for yourself in your life. Your vision board might have people who have had the most successful career that one could possibly have within a finite lifetime, whereas your mother's vision board might have quotes and pictures of people who are able to maintain a nice balance between their family life and work. I hope this conveys the main idea of a vision board to you. So now let's get to why having a vision board is important. A vision board allows you to visualize, which has been known to be one of the most powerful exercises of the mind. If you look around you today, you will see that many people who have succeeded in the fields they have gone in lay great emphasis on visualization. For example, most Olympic athletes have been known to engage their brains in visualization exercises. According to a study published in Psychology Today, when heavy weights are lifted by a weightlifter, the same part of the brain is activated as when the same person just imagines that he or she has lifted some weights.

So what should you be putting on your vision board? You should put anything and everything on your vision board if it is something that motivates and inspires you. If you are unsure about what you find inspiring and motivating, do not be upset. It is only natural for you to feel this way at first. Begin by thinking about what you want to accomplish or what you want to achieve. My vision board had people I looked up to, along with the goals and vision I had in all the areas of my life. Once you gain a general idea of what your future goals are, you will see that they will gradually start taking shape and you will think of more and more things as you go along.

So as I mentioned before, my vision board had a photo of Tony Robbins. If you do not know who Tony Robbins is, let me take a couple of seconds to introduce you to him. Tony Robbins is a motivational speaker, life coach, personal finance coach and the author of various self-help books. His main claim to fame proved to be the infomercials and the number of books he wrote on self-help, such as Unlimited Power, Awaken the Giant Within and Unleash the Power Within. You might also want to know that this brilliant man also made it to the Celebrity 100 list in Forbes magazine in 2007. He makes use of seminars, speeches and written word to talk about his own viewpoint on how one can work on improving their life.

On this photo of Tony Robbins, it said, "Unleashing the Power." I started to look into what type of programs he offered. Tony had a number of different live events and audio programs. I had heard that the man was responsible for changing the lives of many; not only did he do this in a material way, but also in ways that involved helping people change their perspectives. Sometimes, this is all that is needed to make someone feel as they have gone from rags to riches, from having the most unfulfilled and hopeless life to having one of the most fulfilling ones. The one that stood out the most to me was his program called the Ultimate Edge, which is the world's number one bestselling personal and professional achievement system of all time. Tony has worked with millions of people from more than one hundred countries. For the last 36 years, he has been obsessed with finding the difference in the quality of people's lives and why certain people succeed where other people fail. If you pause to think about this, you will be perplexed at the initial absurdity of the ways in which the laws of this universe work, which can sometimes make two people who started off at the same level and put in the same amount of work and effort go two completely different ways. Once you start thinking about it more, you realize that the equation is not so simple. In fact, it is the function of a number of different things that are so diverse in quality and quantity that as much as it seems to be unfair, you begin to realize that it could not be any other way at all. This Ultimate Edge program being carried out by Tony Robbins revealed how you can learn from his obsession with producing immediate results in areas such as your body, emotions, relationships, finances, career, and business.

The Ultimate Edge program changed my life in such a profound way. For once, I felt like I was understood and that I should not feel bad about wanting to succeed. I started to feel and see things differently – and by that I mean that I began to see more things in a positive light. I felt empowered, like I could accomplish anything I wanted. Most importantly, I was getting to know myself better as well as what made me tick in a positive or negative way. I also noticed that things didn't faze me anymore and I took myself out of negative situations at work and in my personal life.

Moreover, within months after taking the program, I finally got my position as a Human Resource Consultant, that I worked hard to work towards and I was told I was the successful candidate for doing corporate human resource training, got a bigger office with big and beautiful windows that brought in allot of natural sunlight. Also, I was told I would be getting an assistant. I got my signing authority and staffing delegating approved by the board of committee who usually grants these delegations. It was so amazing to see how changing the way you think leads to a more optimistic approach towards your life for the better. Whenever I got into a funk, I would go through the whole entire program again just to keep me in check.

Likewise, this man's audio programs were able to do for me what I had not been able to achieve myself. I was able to explore myself in a way that I had never been able to do before. In addition to all this, I was able to understand the different aspects there were to my personality and character. Even small things such as what I liked and disliked now became clearer to me. Through this program, not only was I able to open my eyes to see myself clearly for who I was, but I was also able to regulate myself better because now I had the ability to roughly predict how I would react to a certain thing or whether or not I would like a certain thing or situation.

I believe I went over the entire program five times and will probably go over it again because there was so much that I was able to learn from it. I also felt that there is still more to be gained from this particular program. Furthermore, I now knew that I had to see Tony Robbins live at all cost, because if he was that amazing through his audio programs then he must be phenomenal in person.

In November 2012, I finally got lucky and saw Tony Robbins live in Orlando, Florida. I have to say that it was one of the most amazing experiences in my entire life. It was the first time that I did not feel alone in wanting to succeed and have a life of excellence for myself. I was in the room with 4500 other people wanting the same thing as me. I met so many amazing people from around the world, who were all there to accomplish the same objective. It was interesting to know that we all aspired for the same thing, excellence. Yet we were all coming from such different backgrounds and working towards our aims in such different ways. This again made me realize that what was excellence for me might not be excellence for someone else. Our definitions are very different and we have every right to stick to the definitions that we want to have for ourselves. However, what brought us all together was the fact that we all wanted to venture down the road towards improvement and achieve our own definitions of excellence. This made it a most enriching experience for all of us.

Tony Robbins is a beast. Seeing him live was above and beyond my expectations. I remember walking over burning coals and not feeling a thing. Tony put me in a state where I felt I could achieve and conquer anything. I feel fortunate enough to ever be in that position because anyone who has ever tried to achieve anything similar can tell you how hard it is to feel this way. It is a feat in itself to let yourself go from the shackles of doubt that threaten to bind you to the ground forever, reinforcing the belief that you will never be able to do even half the things you aspired to do or amount to anything at all. Being able to feel that you can conquer and achieve anything at all in this world is a feeling that can propel you in the direction that you have been vying for, all within a single moment.

There was this one moment where we were put in a group of five people. We were asked to close our eyes and count to ten and then open our eyes and point to the person we saw as being a leader. Guess what happened? Three of the five pointed at me, the other pointed at himself, and I was pointing at someone else. That was the turning point for me. At this point is where I realized that other people saw greatness in me, I realized that all along I had been blind too. Prior to this, I never saw myself as a leader or someone who was destined for greatness. I never saw myself heading an important meeting or bringing about any kind of change in the world around me or even in the lives of people I knew so well and was so close to. I do recall several people mentioning to me of my greatness but I didn't internalize it and just thought that they were bullshitting. However, the fact of the matter is that I never took those compliments personally because I did not believe in myself or what I was truly capable of.

And this is where I gave the problem the room and the food it needed in order to grow and flourish within me, slowly eating me away from the inside. My confidence and self-esteem was the main food it fed on and as the feeling of being incapable grew more and more, any hopes I had for myself or my life slowly diminished to nothing. Now I realized just how problematic this had been for me as a person and how much harm it had caused to my life, directly and indirectly.

Had I not had this highly fulfilling experience, I would never have been able to believe in myself. This was the much needed elixir I needed to live, the final attempt at reviving a body that was nothing more than a bunch of organs functioning biologically. Living but not really alive. Isn't that how most of us are? Isn't that how most people see themselves? Ask anyone around you how they feel about their leadership skills and their ability to seek greatness. Be prepared to receive downward glances, embarrassed faces and hesitant stutters as they try to assess what they are capable of and just what they can achieve from in this life.

Brian Tracy says, "We are forever changed by the people we meet and the books we read." I agree with Brian Tracy one hundred and ten percent. I regard everyone I meet as a teacher and every experience as something that I can learn and grow from. For example, a few chapters ago, I spoke about the experience I had with my ex. I could have seen him as another toxic individual in my life (which he actually was), but I could also see him as a teacher of sorts for me, which I also did. He taught me that everyone cannot be trusted and he taught me that I do not need to depend on anyone else for achieving happiness, contentment and greatness. He also taught me that I was whole. I did not need another half. I needed another self-sufficient and well developed whole who could make my life better than it already was and for whom I could do the same.

I became obsessed with personal development and started reading profusely, attending workshops, seminars, and got mentors and coaches to advise and guide me along the way. I can't tell you how important it is to personally develop yourself and create a hunger for it. Your life will be forever changed in such an amazing way and you will wonder why you didn't start sooner. It is just as important that you have the will; it is necessary to have the will to let go of who you were to become who you destined to be: a person destined for greatness. I will warn you that when you start showing up differently in a more positive disposition, people will start to wonder what happened to you and you may even lose a couple of friends in the process. When you start talking about taking your shortcomings or the setbacks you suffer in stride and put a positive spin to any event that would otherwise be seen as negative by the rest of the world, people are going to start to wonder if there is something wrong with your head. They might even begin to feel a little uncomfortable when they come to sit with you and talk to you, so don't be too surprised if they suddenly don't want to hang out with you as often as they used to. Don't feel bad about it because if you grow and people remain the same, you tend to naturally grow apart. It just means that you have to make some other friends with the same outlook; it is important that you have friends with the same outlook so that you can lift each other to new heights. Remember, birds of the same feather flock together; you become the person with whom you spend the most time. Make sure that the people you spend time with the most are those who lift you up rather than tear you down.

CHAPTER 4 – EXERCISE

Check out www.carolbanayos.com/bonuses to complete the Chapter 4 Exercise for Personal Growth and Development.

CHAPTER 5

Forgiveness, Self-Love, Self-Acceptance, and Self-Respect

*"Self-love, self-respect, self-worth.
There is a reason why they all start with 'self.' You cannot find them in anyone else."* Unknown

I'll start off this section of the book by throwing a number of quotes at you. I don't know what or how much you will take from them, but I am hoping you will take away at least a little and that would be better than not taking away anything at all, right?

"Forgiveness is the key that unlocks the door of resentment and the handcuffs of hatred. It is a power that breaks the chains of bitterness and the shackles of selfishness." Come Ten Boom

"I find that when we really love and accept and approve of ourselves exactly as we are, then everything in life works." Louise Hay

"Self-respect cannot be hunted. It cannot be purchased. It is never for sale. It cannot be fabricated out of public relations. It comes to us when we are alone, in quiet moments, in quiet places, when we suddenly realize that, knowing the good, we have done it; knowing the beautiful, we have served it; knowing the truth we have spoken it." Alfred Whitney Griswold

As I moved towards a stage where my conscious awareness was now awake and as I moved away from my state of stupor, I began to learn more about forgiveness. When I talk about forgiveness, I am not just talking about forgiveness for others, but I am also referring here to the forgiveness that one sometimes needs to extend to the self.

I hear you questioning me right now, and rightly so, I suppose. I, too, did not realize the important of forgiving oneself until I managed to accomplish a significant part of this journey to conscious awareness. So why is it important to forgive yourself? Sometimes you do not know how much harm you are causing to yourself by holding so much against your own self. Initially, when I was still in my zombie-like state, I also didn't realize how much hatred I had towards myself and the amount of negative self-talk going on in my mind. I don't know whether you are aware of this or not (and if you are not, then here comes another life lesson for you, my dear reader), but self-talk can have a profound impact on the way you think and on your actions.

Essentially, self-talk can play a fundamental role in determining who you are. It factors in to a very large extent when determining how confident a person is or whether a person has low self-esteem or high self-esteem. Now that you know what self-talk is in a nutshell, let's move on. So my self-talk was fairly negative, as I have already mentioned. The things I used to say to myself were phrases or sentences that would hurt anyone. I constantly told myself that I was stupid, I was not attractive, I was not worthy of doing any good, I was nothing more than a failure, I could not possibly achieve anything good in life, I was not as active as I should be, and I was simply just not good enough. It does not really take a genius to figure out that these sayings had a very negative impact on my self-worth and my self-confidence was virtually nonexistent. What makes such negative self-talk really bad is that it becomes sort of like a self-fulfilling prophecy or a vicious cycle. For example, I told myself I could not amount to anything worthwhile and this broke away at my self-confidence. As my self-confidence lowered, it made me tell myself that I was useless and worthless once more.

For a person who was in my position, the journey to conscious awareness is nothing short of a life saver. As I learned more about forgiveness and the importance of forgiveness, I began to heal. When I decided to forgive myself, I broke down in tears. I have to say that this was one of the most amazing feelings that one could possibly have. When I forgave myself for all my flaws and shortcomings, I felt more loved. As I released myself from this prison of hatred that I had shut myself in, being and accepting who I truly was made more sense to me than ever before. Once I forgave myself, it was easier to forgive other people. Mahatma Gandhi says, "The weak can never forgive. Forgiveness is the attribute of the strong."

I decided to also forgive my parents. In my Asian and Filipino culture, parents play a very important role in the upbringing of a child and a child is never allowed to disobey their parents. Basically, the parents of any child hold the ultimate power in his or her life and their word is law. It is also normal for parents to physically beat and hit their children as a form of discipline. Since I was a child, I was physically beaten and hit by my father for misbehaving or doing things he didn't like. This continued until I was about twenty-two. I can only recall a few times where I was physically beaten by my mother.

Looking back, I can think of a number of different incidents where I was punished in such a way that it almost seems a little hard to believe now. Chances are that you probably have not been through the same, so my parents might seem a little more draconian to you than they did to me. Unless, you are from an Asian or Filipino background, of course. I can recall a time when my siblings and I had to march on the coffee table and if our knees didn't go high enough, we would get whipped with a leather belt. This was just because my dad felt like it, it was not the result of discipline. I remember once calling my dad a "fucking asshole" because he was so strict and mean, and, man, did I ever get it.

My siblings and I were also held prisoners in our house because my dad didn't want us to go out. It was during the summer so it was really hard to stay inside. Being the rebellious child that I was, I decided to sneak out and go for a bike ride. When I got home, I was beaten very badly. The weird thing is that I became numb to the beatings and still remember saying, "Is that all you got?" There was also a time when I had my driving test but I wasn't allowed to leave the house. I snuck out and took my dad's car to the test. Not only did I get the beats, but my television and stereo were smashed along with all my clothes being thrown into the big garbage bin. I had to wait for my dad to leave so I could pick through the garbage and take back my clothes. I did pass my driver's test in the end, so to me it was still worth it. To be honest, I could probably write a whole separate book for what my siblings and mother had to go through. There were several occasions where we had to call the police and get my dad hospitalized and put in the psych ward because he reacted in such inhumane ways. I was so angry at my mother for always taking him back despite his behavior and hated her for not protecting her children from her violent husband.

CAROL BANAYOS

During my childhood, I don't remember my parents ever showing any feelings of love, safety or security. My siblings and I were never told that we were loved and were never shown any comfort or affection like hugs and kisses. As a result, we were never taught what real love was or taught how to properly deal with and express our feelings. Therefore, my feelings became suppressed and, as a result, was the cause behind my inability to express my feeling and emotions. I feel that the kind of environment I grew up in also contributed to my lack of confidence and self-worth. Because I always saw my mother taking my father back despite the way he treated her and his children, I guess I grew up with the idea that you have to put up with everything and you can never say no. Deep down inside, I might have believed that giving up on a relationship is a failure or maybe it was not an option at all, since that is what my mother's actions conveyed. As a result of this, I grew up without the strength that one needs to walk away from a toxic relationship.

I had to come to an understanding that maybe it was because of the way my parents were brought up that my siblings and I were raised and treated the way we were. After all, most people grow up to be exactly like their parents and my parents were not given an easy time by their parents either. For example, both my parents were physically beaten and hit by their parents. My dad almost killed his father with a shotgun because he cheated on his mother and left her to raise all the children alone.

So it seems like violence was an acceptable reaction in the household for him because that is exactly what he saw when he was growing up as well. Still, my father didn't always beat us. There was a time when we were very young that he took care of us. So why did this change?

My dad's mother was moving to Winnipeg from the Philippines and a week before she was supposed to arrive, she died. And my dad has never been the same since. Both my parents did the best they could with what tools they were given. With that perspective and understanding, I learned to forgive them. Please do not think even for a second that my forgiving them means that I was okay with what they did. I am not saying what they did was right because I know that it was not. I just knew that I had to accept it for what it was. I could not view their behavior or the way they raised us in isolation; if I did that, it would make them seem like nothing more than tyrants. I mean, you just read the ways I was punished for my insolence and rebellious behavior as a child. Does that happen in every household? Is that how all parents discipline their children? I don't think so. Yes, parents need to discipline their children, but sometimes a kind word or two can be more productive than a slap or a whipping. However, as I grew older, I realized that the fault was not within my parents. When you grow up with a certain lifestyle, you gradually begin to accept it. You begin to think that it is okay to behave in a certain way. In my parents' case, violence was an acceptable part of the equation for any relationship. As Eckhart Tolle says, "We have to accept suffering before we can transcend it." This I had to transcend and with this transcendence came a sense of lightness and ease with the ability to forgive others.

I realized that by holding all this anger and pain, I became numb to what was going on around me. I also began to emulate my parents in every way, just like they had copied their own parents. This meant that I would often find myself in a situation or in a relationship that was doing me more harm than good. So what did I do? Just like my mother, I also put up with it. When we are lacking the love, safety and comfort that we need to grow, survive and live in this world, we tend to seek that comfort from others, which may end up hurting us more in the long run. This is because, for one, they are not capable of providing us with the things we need. We then come to terms that this sense of love, comfort, and safety needs to come from within us. We must have self-love for ourselves first in order to know what true love is, and it is only when we love ourselves that we will attract the person who is worthy of us. The first step towards self-love is our ability to forgive ourselves and forgive others. Steve Maraboli says, "Love yourself. Forgive yourself. Be true to yourself. How you treat yourself sets the standard for how others will treat you." He is right.

What I am saying might seem to be confusing or fluff-like. There is no set number of steps that you have to follow to reach this step. There are no guidelines; different people reach this point in life through very different ways and because of very different reasons. However, what ultimately matters is whether you are able to achieve this point or not. My purpose of sharing bits and pieces of my own background is to provide you with an example. An example of how things can be and how things can also change. I hope that at least a handful of people who are reading my story will be able to seek inspiration from what I am trying to tell you and pick up a few pieces of advice here and there.

If you constantly dwell on your flaws and faults and blame yourself for everything that seems to go wrong in your life, you will be wasting a lot of energy that you could, instead, channel into something that is more productive. When you do not forgive yourself, you live in the fear of your own vulnerability and continue to burn with anger because of whatever it is that is causing you pain. As a result of this, there is a constant mood of sadness, blame, and hurt. However, it is your right and your duty to put this energy into something out of which you can gain something positive. Feed your abilities and your creativity with that energy, not negativity. Once you are able to forgive yourself, you will find yourself living in the here and now instead of living in the past. As a result of this, you can gradually progress into the future with a renewed purpose in life, one that is focused primarily on improvement, growth, and change. Instead of being held back by the hurtful memories of the past, you can continue to build on your experiences in life.

So why don't people forgive themselves? Well, there are a number of reasons for this. When you have been blaming yourself for so long, you build your own sense of self on vulnerability, resentment and anger. If you stop blaming yourself, you might fear that you will lose your sense of self. However, stop yourself at this point and ask yourself some very simple questions: is this who you really are? Is this the identity that you want to live with for the rest of your life? Is this the kind of person you want to be known as by those around you? Is it really worth it to dwell only on the negative and never focus on the positive? Is it actually making anything better or is it only causing you harm? Trust me, more often than not, this will only be hurting and harming you. Given that this is so, is it really worth all the effort? You are allowed to be insecure and you are allowed to think that certain things might be hard for you to achieve. However, instead of saying that one failure means you can never achieve anything in life, learn to see that as a challenge and let that be a driving force that motivates you to become even bigger and better than what you were before.

If you continue to blame yourself, you will eventually find out that you are doing nothing but harming yourself emotionally and physically. In most cases, people are often filled with anger and resentment, which makes it difficult for them to overcome their inability to forgive themselves. A number of studies have been carried out to study the link between resentment and anger and the health of the individual. The results of all of these studies have shown that the more resentful and angrier you are, the more likely you are to suffer from various types of diseases.

When I say that you need to forgive yourself, I am not saying you need to turn a blind eye on your weaknesses or on all your failures in the past. Take my example: when I forgave my parents, however, I have been treated suitably during my childhood. I did not say that what they did was wrong. I only explored the causes that led to them treating their children in a certain manner and understood that they could be forgiven for this. Similarly, you can apply this to yourself too. Instead of forgetting the unfortunate experiences that you have had to go through in the past, look at them as learning experiences. Let those experiences guide you. Explore the causes behind those unfortunate events and think about how you could attempt to change those. Think about the effect these events had on you and recall how you could have reacted instead. This way, as you compare both scenarios, you will deal with them in a better way.

I understand that this process is not always easy. In fact, I can tell you that it is not easy at all. You will undergo all sorts of emotions to a heightened extent. However, you need to learn to accept those emotions. Accept the anger that will erupt within you when you think of the way others treated you unfairly. Accept the resentment you will have of yourself for the way you behaved that caused your failure. Identify what the problem is and accept that it is, indeed, a problem. Once you are ready to identify the problem and accept the cluster of emotions that come rushing in, you will find yourself in a much better position with regards to forgiving yourself.

When we learn to forgive ourselves and when we learn to love ourselves, we also figure out how to accept ourselves for who we are and respect ourselves for the individuals we are today. We learn to accept where we are today and know we are at this point in time in our life for a reason. If we are not happy where we currently are in life, it is up us to change it for the better by striving to new heights and becoming that person we always dreamt of becoming. We are all such amazing human beings capable of anything we put our mind to and once we realize that, we can become our own role model and admire ourselves for all the skills, abilities, and qualities that we embody. Mahatma Gandhi says, "Self-respect has no considerations." Clint Eastwood also says beautifully, "Respect your efforts, respect yourself. Self-respect leads to self-discipline. When you have both firmly under your belt, that's real power."

It has been said that, "once you are able to accept and respect yourself for who you are, and learn to forgive while loving yourself, only then can you find real self-love."

So now do you want to know what self-love looks like? Self-love is when you give priority to your dreams and make an effort to engage in activities and seek out situations that are truly inspiring for you. Self-love means that you will know that you have the right and the ability to decline or reject opinions, suggestions or situations that you are uncomfortable with or that are not in line with your beliefs.

When you love yourself, you will automatically find yourself looking out for people who motivate you and support you to become the best you can be. It also gives you the courage to experience all those moments that you have dreamed of experiencing. It gives you the power to accept your own thoughts and opinions. It gives you the strength to stand strong in the face of what you believe in and not be swayed to follow the opinion of the masses.

Self-love also plays a role in helping you be kind to yourself. It helps you realize that it is okay to take out time to nourish your soul, mind and body by engaging in healthy exercise, eating healthy food and sometimes just giving yourself some time alone.

Self-love encourages you to honor your truth and to trust your intuition. It gives you the courage to believe in yourself, to believe that you are capable of bringing to life what you have always dreamed of. Self-love allows you to tell yourself that there is no obstacle that is insurmountable and that you are capable of doing anything that you set your heart to. It gives you the little boost that needs to come from within if you have to do something on your own. It allows you to accept yourself for who you are. Qualities, flaws, quirks, and all.

But what is love? If you ask five different people to define love, chances are that you will end up with five different answers. Because most people choose to define love in different ways, it means that they end up showing their love in different ways as well. Zick Rubin, a social psychologist, says that there are three main aspects to what we call love, which are intimacy, attachment, and caring.

But wait a minute? Is the love you feel for your significant other the same love you feel for your mother or your friend or your pet? No, you're right. It isn't. It sometimes becomes quite hard to understand the complicated emotion that is love. And there are different forms of love. Different forms of love are expressed in different ways and encompass different aspects.

Different relationships have different boundaries, characteristics and dynamics. Different relationships involve different levels of intimacy.

What you consider to be intimate can also differ from one relationship to another. For example, you may consider intimacy to be affectionate or sexual, or you may think that intimacy means to be able to trust the other person (as in the case of a friendship).

Typically, a romantic relationship will include all these aspects. The relationships you have with your family members and friends, on the other hand, will usually be based more on trust and affection. The purpose of intimacy is to allow both individuals in the relationship to effectively and respectfully communicate with each other and to treat each other as equals.

Different relationships also have different levels of commitment. For example, in a marital relationship, the two individuals will probably commit to monogamy. If you have just started dating someone, you might place loyalty to your friends and family above loyalty to your new partner. Some people might always choose to give more priority to their commitment to partners, or family members over their friends. It basically varies from person to person as well. In general, however, it is seen that most people tend to value their commitment to their romantic partners and family more than their friendships.

There are some commonalities that can be drawn between the different types of love and some attributes are found in almost all relationships (or even if they are not found, they should ideally be there). For example, you will want your partner to care for you, you will want your mother to care for you and you will want your friend to care for you. What does this show? Caring is an aspect that is shared by all these different forms of love. Another common attribute is that of devotion.

There are also a couple of negative aspects that are common to all types of love. For example, whether you are friends with someone or whether you have been dating someone for a long time, you may feel betrayed or mistreated by the other person at times, or you may feel pressurized or threatened by the risk of rejection.

I feel that a healthy relationship can only exist between two people who are comfortable with themselves on their own, in addition to being comfortable with each other. You can only attain love once you know that your own happiness should be your top priority. Most of us are so scared to come to terms with the many flaws that we have and to admit that we have faults is not an easy task for many.

Because of this, we end up falling in love with other people and forming relationships with them for all the wrong reasons. Some people do it to battle the crippling loneliness, others feel that it is the right time for them to settle down, while another set of people simply seek out relationships because they feel that being with someone is going to help in easing away the pain that other life's obstacles have caused them.

However, happiness can only be meaningful when it comes about as a result of an individual working hard towards becoming the individual that he or she wants to be. Through self-growth, one can become more aware of his or her own desires. At the same time, this will also allow you to have more realistic expectations of who your ideal partner is. For this, it is okay to be selfish and focus only on yourself.

When you are able to love and respect yourself, you free yourself from unnecessary doubt and worry. You learn to trust your own decisions and feelings. You become more authentic and you become more courageous. You let yourself live from the heart and enjoy a life that is more generous. A life that is bigger and kinder. You set yourself free from your self-imposed reins and you get the courage to dream big.

When you love yourself, you are able to let go of the negativity that surrounds you and focus more on all the beauty that is also present alongside it. Instead of focusing on all the doors that have closed or are closing for you, you choose to look at all the endless possibilities that await you. You become grateful for where you are in life and everything that you have been blessed with.

My own experience has shown me that you begin to emanate confidence, positivity, peace, happiness and playfulness as a result of this. These qualities and emotions attract others to you, like iron nails to a horseshoe magnet. Just like that, you will find your ideal partner drawn towards you. It will be natural, it will be free, and it will be fulfilling.

CHAPTER 5 – EXERCISE

Check out www.carolbanayos.com/bonuses to complete the Chapter 5 Exercise for Forgiveness, Self-Love, Self-Acceptance, and Self-Respect.

CHAPTER 6

Health, Veganism, and the Many Benefits of Adopting a Plant-Based Diet

"He who has health, has hope; and he who has hope, has everything." Thomas Carlyle

"The doctor of the future will no longer treat the human frame with drugs, but rather will cure and prevent disease with nutrition." Thomas Edison

How does health factor into the process of awakening?

My awakening and conscious awareness led me to start looking at my health and thinking about what I could do to enhance it, since I believe that health is the true wealth. There is no purpose of achieving our goals and being successful when our health is suffering. I mean, can you really enjoy life and all its luxuries if your body isn't even functioning properly? A.J. Reb Materi says, "So many people spend their health gaining wealth, and then have to spend their wealth to regain their health." Even Herophilus states, "When health is absent, wisdom cannot reveal itself, art cannot manifest itself, strength cannot fight, wealth becomes useless, and intelligence cannot be applied."

Approximately three years ago, I decided to stop eating meat. I truly believe that when we eat the flesh and meat of animals, we also take in all the pain and suffering that they endured in the process. It is no different to when a person receives a transplant from a complete stranger and they begin displaying the same skills, characteristics, memories and feelings from their donor. Mohandas K. Gandhi says, "I do not regard flesh food as necessary for us. I hold flesh food to be unsuited to our species. To my mind, the life of a lamb is no less precious than that of a human being. I should be unwilling to take the life of a lamb for the sake of the human body. The more helpless the creature, the more it is entitled to protection from human and from the cruelty of humans."

My research into the meat, dairy and eggs industry has showed that there is a high correlation with the consumption of these products and the top fifteen causes of death. According to the World Health Organization, dietary factors contribute to at least thirty percent of all cases of cancers in the Western world. The cancer researchers noted that people who did not consume a lot of meat or did not eat it altogether were much less likely to develop cancer. Studies were carried out in Germany and England that show that vegetarians have a 40 percent lower risk of developing cancer as opposed to those individuals who regularly eat meat. There may be a number of different reasons. For example, meat does not contain the nutrients or fiber content that serves a protective factor against cancer. Meat also has lots of animal proteins, carcinogenic compounds and saturated fats. Furthermore, it was found that because meat has a high fat content, it leads to an increase in the production of hormones, which leads to an increase in the risk of cancers related to hormones, such as prostate cancer and breast cancer.

According to Dr. Gregor's informative video, Uprooting the Leading Causes of Death, the number one cause of death in the United States is heart disease, which is caused due to high levels of cholesterol in the blood according to the Harvard Nurses' Health Study, which studied the Risk Factors for Mortality. The study is a Competing Risks Analysis study, which means that it compared different risk factors. According to this study, consuming the amount of cholesterol that is found in just a single egg that is had everyday cuts a woman's life short by the same amount as smoking five cigarettes a day for fifteen years would. Still think eggs are healthy? The most protective behaviour according to this study was consuming fiber. Having a cup of oatmeal, for example, can have the same positive impact on extending a woman's life as jogging for four hours everyday for a week would. You can clearly figure out what the effect of an animal based diet is going to be, as compared to a plant-based diet; while an animal based diet was associated with a shortening of women's lives, a plant-based diet was associated with an extension of a woman's life.

It all started on my 11th birthday, when I was on an island in the Philippines and it was decided that there was to be a big feast in celebration of my birthday. During the preparation of that feast, I witnessed my family members kill a pig, goat, sheep and cow, as well as some chickens. It was one of most horrific things I have ever experienced. I can still hear the loud noises from the pig as its neck was being sliced open. I stopped eating meat automatically and for the rest of my time there, which was two months, I only ate potatoes, tomatoes and fruit. When I got back home, I continued to refuse meat. I did love McDonald's, especially the Big Mac, but I would have it without the meat. My family was telling me that I could not survive and that I had to start eating meat again for the protein. I eventually started eating meat again. Throughout the years, I have been off and on with eating meat.

I finally decided to quit cold turkey in 2012 after attending an event on a related subject and watching a documentary called Earthlings. My compassion towards animals was a strong leading factor and I did not care what my family or friends would think or say to me this time. I made a decision, and no one was to going change my mind or talk me out of it. Luckily, my family and friends were now more accepting, which made the transition from meat eater to non-meat eater easier.

In 2014, I decided that I would go vegan but I did have the occasional slip-ups with dairy, specifically cheese and ice cream. My research led me to a speech by Gary Yourofsky where I learned about the atrocities that animals in the dairy and egg industry had to endure, which was much more horrific than the meat industry. I did not want to be part of anything that would cause harm or suffering to animals just to satisfy my appetite. I chose to eliminate those slip-ups right after my research. Also, since 2014, I have not bought any leather, wool, silk or down. However, I do have leather products and down from before I decided to go vegan, which I will wear out or give away.

Many people ask me what a vegan is and the best explanation I could find was to describe a vegan as a person who avoids using and consuming animals and animal products for any purpose, including food, clothing, and entertainment. I believe there is a huge detachment with the packaged dairy, egg and meat products that we see in our grocery stores. I don't think we stop to think that these were once living beings, or how and what these animals had to endure in order to become these packaged products. These animals who are sentient beings, have been turned into commodities that can be bought and sold like copper and coffee. They are no different to the cats and dogs that we have chosen to call our pets. We have just been conditioned to reduce chickens, pigs and cows along with other animals as non-beings, non-sentient. It breaks my heart and brings me to tears when I think of what these animals have to go through. If we are willing to eat meat, dairy, and eggs, we need to become aware of how it is being produced along with the billions of animals that are being killed for these industries each year. We also need to become aware of how it impacts the human population, land and marine animals, water, rainforests, and our planet as a whole.

I personally feel that becoming vegan was not just about changing my diet. For me, it became like a new philosophy that I had adopted; I can definitely say that there was a substantial change in my lifestyle that accompanied this new philosophy of mine. You may choose to become vegan for any reason. For example, like me, the ethical aspect may play a big role in convincing you to adopt this change.

At this point, let me take a moment to point out that veganism and vegetarianism are not the same thing. I will try to put this down in simple words. For starters, a person who is a vegan will generally not eat any kind of food item that has any animal origins. For example, even honey is not part of the diet of a strict vegan because it comes from bees. On the other hand, a person who is a vegetarian may be quite comfortable with having dairy products and eggs.

In addition to not consuming anything that comes from animals, vegans do not use any other products that are made from animals. For example, wearing leather jackets, lamb wool sweaters or down jackets is out of the question for vegans. Furthermore, they will not use any cosmetics that contain products obtained from animals or if they have been tested on animals. Soaps and silk are commonly avoided by vegans.

The most common reason why people become vegans is because they support the rights of animals. Although eggs and milk are not obtained by killing animals, vegans still do not consume them. This is because vegans believe that, just like humans, animals also have the right to live freely and humans should not interfere with their lifestyles. For example, in today's day and age, it is common practice for commercial farmers to feed their animals with food that has been infused with growth hormones so that they grow faster, produce more milk or lay larger eggs. What happens is that most of these animals, such as cows and chickens, are ready to be slaughtered once they are no longer as productive as the farmer wants them to be. The way that farming has evolved over time means that animals are given more chemicals and substance to make them grow unnaturally.

In addition to this, vegans also believe that livestock farming has a horrible effect on the environment. The production of food from animal farming is very inefficient; just producing all the animal feed that is required for these animals means that a lot of land is taken up and a lot of other important resources are also used, such as water and fertilizers. These resources could, instead, be used to feed the hundreds and thousands of humans that go hungry every day. Livestock farming has also led to an increase in topsoil erosion, which means that the land is no longer as productive for the cultivation of crops as it used to be. Many forests have been turned into farmlands and grazing areas for cattle while most water sources (including groundwater) have been polluted because of animal waste that runs down into them from farms and feeding areas.

To the effect of a documentary called 'Cowspiracy', you can see the uncovering of the destructive industry of animal agriculture. This leads to causes of pollution and water consumption. Not only is it responsible for emitting more greenhouse gases as compared to the transportation industry, but it also causes topsoil erosion and makes any environment ill. Similarly, according to World Watch Institute, 51% of Green House Gas emission is caused by animal agriculture.

WAKE THE FUCK UP

Cowspiracy is as inspiring and eye opening as 'An Inconvenient Truth' and 'Blackfish.' This documentary unfolds the devastation large-scale farming brings, though it also paves ways towards global sustainability for growing populations. Cowspiracy says that eating 1 hamburger require 660 gallons of water to produce which is equivalent to 2 months of showering. Likewise, 1 pound of meat requires 2520 gallons of water to produce. It is interesting to note that the impact of livestock, animal agriculture emits 65% nitrous oxide, causing up to 51% human climate change, 30% global consumption while consuming 45% of land. The land use leads to 91% of Brazilian forest destruction, causing ocean dead zone. Moreover, habitat destruction and species extinction follow up naturally as a result.

It is estimated that ¾ of the fishery is over exploded and will be non-existence by 2048. For every 1 pound of fish that is caught, 5 pounds of untargeted wild fish are caught as well which is called by-kill.

Meanwhile, for every 1 acre of land you can produce 37,000 pounds of vegetables. This adds to a positive impact where for every 1 acre of land you can only produce 375 pounds of meat.

Healthily, by adopting a plant-based diet you can per day save 1100 gallons of water, 45 pounds of grain, 30 square foot of forest, 10 pounds of CO_2, and save one animal's life.

Health benefits are, of course, a major reason why people have turned towards veganism. If your diet is made up mostly of proteins and animal fats, there is a larger risk of developing diseases like rheumatoid arthritis, diabetes, hypertension and cancer. For example, cow's milk is commonly consumed across the world but many vegans believe that it is not actually produced for consumption by humans because its content of fat and protein is very different from what is required by humans.

A study published in the Journal of Urology showed that if a man who has been diagnosed with early-stage prostate cancer changes his lifestyle and diet to a plant based diet, it is possible for him to actually prevent the illness from worsening. In fact, it might even be possible to reverse the illness altogether. Another study carried out in the United States that involved more than half a million individuals. The results of this study showed that people who consume a lot of processed meat or red meat are much more likely to die prematurely than those who don't. In October 2012, an article was published in Food Technology; according to the article, individuals with a plant-based diet can actually counter their genetic predisposition towards the development of certain diseases, such as cancer, type III diabetes and cardiovascular issues.

What is a plant-based diet? A plant-based diet is one that is rich in whole-grains, fruits and vegetables. Legumes, for example, do not contain any cholesterol and are very low in saturated fats. In addition to this, they are also a rich source of fiber and several other nutrients. Instead of consuming dairy products, you can obtain proteins from a number of plant-based products, such as soya, beans and peanuts.

There are a number of benefits to be had from this kind of diet. By cutting down on dairy products and meat items, you reduce the amount of saturated fats that you are consuming. This means that you lower the risk of developing heart diseases. Most plant-based foods contain the right amount of carbohydrates that are needed by the body. Contrary to what a lot of people have been blinded into believing, you *do* need carbohydrates because they provide you with the energy that the brain needs to function properly. Without any carbohydrates, you will not be able to use your brain to its proper potential. Most fruits and vegetables also contain the right amount of fiber that can lead to healthier bowel movements. Not only does this protect you from colon cancer, but it also prevents regular problems like constipation and leaves you feeling healthy and light.

Plant-based foods are also rich in magnesium and potassium. Magnesium helps the body to absorb calcium and is usually found in food like leafy green vegetables, seeds and nuts. Potassium is needed by the body to balance the acidity and water level. It also plays an important role in helping the kidneys to eliminate toxins. Research also suggests that it lowers the risk of cancer and cardiovascular diseases. Antioxidants are also found in plant-based foods. They protect the body from cell damage; some studies have also shown that they might also help in preventing cancer. Furthermore, anti-oxidants will give you healthy and glowing skin. Clean skin and a healthy body, what more could you want?

With the alarming rise in heart disease and obesity alongside regular reports of people claiming to be hypertensive or have high cholesterol levels, one really needs to sit down and reconsider their lifestyle and diet. A high consumption of meat items and dairy products is harmful in more ways than one. Meat and dairy products contain a lot of saturated fats, which can have a negative impact on the cardiovascular system of the body. In addition to this, numerous medical studies have shown that this also leads to an increase in blood pressure and damages the arteries. Not to mention, dairy products and meat are also high in cholesterol and calories. With increased stress and reduced activity, it becomes difficult for the body to deal with all the excess intake of cholesterol.

A lot of fat is found in meat items, making them a source of excessive calories. This can easily cause a person to gain extra weight if there is no exercise to balance it out. When you cook meat, a lot of carcinogenic compounds are also produced. Also, the consumption of meat has been directly shown to lead to an increased risk of colon cancer because meat is deposited in the intestines and is only removed when a person ingests an ample amount of fiber. This is because protein-rich meat items take longer to be digested by the body and, therefore, remain in the intestines for a longer period of time, during which the carcinogenic compounds can easily damage the intestinal walls. A lot of people with diets comprising mostly of meat items and dairy products also complain about having troubles with digestion. The reason for this is that meat passes along the intestines extremely slowly, so it gradually putrefies. This means that a lot of amines and toxins are produced and accumulated in the kidneys, large intestines and liver. This leads to a number of digestive problems, such as stomach cramps, constipation and hemorrhoids.

A lifestyle change is needed in this situation. By that, I don't only mean a change in diet; you also need to incorporate a healthy exercise regimen into your everyday routine. You don't need to get a super expensive gym membership and hire your own personal trainer, neither do you need to invest in a home gym and buy the most expensive equipment around. All you need to do is take out fifteen to thirty minutes every day. Maybe before you hurry off to work or just before dinner for a small set of exercise steps that you can do in the comfort of your own home. You can look around online for various exercise plans as well. Alternatively, if you prefer fresh air, you could also go out for a brisk walk or a jog, given that the weather and location allows you to do so. As most of you already know, exercise is a great way to lose weight because you burn a lot of calories. You do not need to worry about high blood pressure or heart disease, because engaging in regular exercise will boost the production of "good" cholesterol that allows smooth blood flow around the body. Through regular exercise, you can prevent many different health issues, such as metabolic syndrome, depression, cancer, stroke and arthritis.

If you think that switching over to a plant-based diet is not going to provide you with the energy you need to function, think again. If you indulge yourself in fruits such as apples, oranges and berries, which are absolutely chock full of natural sugars, you can expect to get the same kind of boost you would otherwise get from caffeine. Furthermore, most fruits are loaded with vitamin C, which is needed for energy and also battles fatigue. So a plant-based diet can give you the boost and all the energy that you need to work out on a regular basis. Just because you are not having meat or animal based food items day and night does not mean that your body is missing out on any of the nutrients that it needs. Don't worry for a second about not getting the required level of protein. Adult men usually need around fifty-six grams of protein each day, while women need around forty-six grams, according to the 'Vegetarian Resource Group'. It gives you a clearer perspective on the recommended amount of intake of protein on a daily basis to adopt the vegan diet in the long run. This gives you freedom of choice in your consumption of a variety of vegetables, beans and legumes as your main source of protein.

Exercise is also a great way of improving your mood. If you are ever looking for an emotional uplift or want to release your anger or exhaustion after a long day at work, I would suggest going for a jog or hitting the gym. Physical activity leads to the production of feel-good hormones that make people feel much more relaxed and happier. Give it a try just once and I promise that you will leave feeling much better about yourself and your appearance. I have personally found this to be a great way to improve my self-confidence and to boost my self-esteem. In addition to this, you can also enhance your endurance and increase muscle strength through exercise. This is because it helps in delivering nutrients and oxygen to the body tissues, which allows the body to work in a more efficient manner.

CHAPTER 6 – EXERCISE

Check out www.carolbanayos.com/bonuses to complete the Chapter 6 Exercise for Health and the Many Benefits of Adopting a Plant-Based Diet.

CHAPTER 7

Resilience and Inner Strength

"I'm strong because I've been weak. I'm brave because I've been afraid. I'm wise because I've been foolish." Unknown

Life throws many curveballs at us. At different stages in life, we undergo different catastrophes and stresses. To be resilient does not mean that we sail through life without ever coming across any obstacle or hurdle. To be resilient simply means that we are able to stand strong in the face of such distress in times and not fall back. We may express our grief or sadness, but we also remain standing and do not give up. Having a positive view of the self and having confidence in one's strengths and abilities can build up one's resilience, as can healthy relationships with friends and family members.

What is inner strength? Here is what Aarti Khurana has to say on the subject:

"Every woman has infinite potential to achieve anything she wants. She just needs to stop underestimating herself and discover her true inner strength. She will find within her an unlimited capacity to achieve."

Inner strength is a term that is often used in place of resilience. It can be taken to mean one's mental resistance to discouragement, doubt and negativity. It is also used to refer to how resolute an individual is. An individual with greater inner strength will be more resolute about what he or she believes in and what he or she wants from life as opposed to one who does not possess the same level of inner strength.

I had a mental shift, what you can call an "Ah-ha!" moment, with my awakening of conscious awareness. I came to realize that the hardship and struggles I had experienced in my life were helping me to build the resilience and inner strength that I should have had right from the start and that I needed to grow and develop and transform as an individual.

As a result of this, my capacity to deal with challenging and stressful situations became somewhat easy. Situations that I would previously worry about and stress over became non-existent for me; this was mainly because I realized that there was absolutely no need to worry. I am happy that I developed an attitude of "This too shall pass." This is only because I came to understand that all these hardships were temporary and would not last forever. It only lasted forever if I chose to dwell upon it.

Let's try looking at an example. If you are down with the flu or something else, you can continuously think about it and make yourself worse than you already do thanks to your condition. However, if you choose to ignore it instead and busy yourself with other work, chances are that you won't even have time to blink before your pain and misery is over. This example might seem a little silly to you right now, but you need to be able to extract the lesson that I am trying to convey through this and apply it to everyday life situations. Do not think that one bad thing is going to signal the end of the world, because it's not. To put it simply, things are bound to get better because that is the trajectory of this rollercoaster called life.

Also, I found out that I was much stronger than I thought I was. Each experience I had was developing my emotional muscle of resilience and inner strength. "Strength does not come from winning. Your struggles develop your strengths. When you go through hardship and decide not to surrender, that is strength."

I recently read a quote that goes something like this: "Life is like photography. We develop from the negatives." This quote is true to an extent. I believe we can develop from the negatives if we decide to do two things. First, we need to learn how to see ourselves as a victor rather than just a poor victim of our own circumstances. Second, this will enable us to view the negative experiences as learning experiences instead, which will allow us to grow as individuals since we can learn from the mistakes that we have made in the past. When negative things happen in our lives, it is easy to become a victim of your circumstance. It is easy to start blaming yourself for what is going wrong. It is also easy to say that life is unfair, that the world is out to get you, and that everything always seems to be going wrong for you while the people around you are succeeding. You can't seem to think clearly and get caught up in all the bullshit. It's like a constant force is pulling you down into the throes of sadness and despair. Then, before you know it, the self-sabotage and pity parties kick in. What you will notice is that misery loves company, and you will always find someone who will console you and validate that you are a victim to join in the pity party.

What you need to learn at this time is that bad things happen to everyone. Just because your neighbor smiles and whistles on his way to work while you glumly lock your door and slowly trudge down the road to catch the bus does not mean that you are the only one having a bad time. Yes, it is true that some people have had to see a greater number of painful events or adversity as opposed to others and yes, that does make you wonder why it's happening to you. Trust me, I have been there myself. However, the only thing I can say at this point is that life really is not fair. Bad things happen and they affect us sooner or later. You will feel like crying and you will want to feel sorry for yourself and you will want others to feel sorry for you. In fact, if they don't, you might also get angry. Can't they see how much pain you are in? Don't they realize how hard life has been for you?

However, at a certain point, you need to stop thinking about the past. Stop thinking about things that bothered you and don't let them get to you anymore. If you don't do this, you will not be able to progress forwards or grow and function in a constructive and productive way. What is it about self-pity that is problematic? Well, the first thing that is highly problematic about this is that self-pity comes about purely by our own choice. We let it develop to an extent where it takes control over our lives. At this point, remember that you are only being self-absorbed. You continue living in this destructive cycle where you dwell on the negative aspects of life and you try to move about and carry on with life by bringing all that resentment and bitterness with you. When you keep thinking about the negative aspects, you lose focus of your life and you stop even trying to regain control. So you need to stop playing the blame game. Stop blaming the bad things that happen in your life for the position you are at in life today because this just goes to show that you have given up all control and responsibility. Remember, everything in this world is a result of the choice we make. This means that you can choose to keep on spreading your misery or you can also choose to rise and move beyond your circumstances. When you indulge yourself in self-pity, you stop thinking about the suffering and needs of others. In this state, the only thing you care about is your own suffering.

When I researched my coaches' and mentor's past, I was surprised that they all had been through horrific, difficult and very negative experiences throughout their lives. I believe that is the reason why I resonated with them so well. I felt the pain they had gone through and struggles of their life stories, and I admired their strength and conviction towards their goals.

I have already talked about the harsh ways that my father used to discipline us at home. That was not the only reason why I now say that I did not have an easy childhood. My siblings and I grew up in a pretty rough neighborhood, the kind of place that you would not want to visit or walk through alone. This is the North End of the city, which people commonly refer to as the ghetto.

At that point in time, life was such that we found ourselves living in the core of a region where everything "bad" or illegal took place. You could see drug dealers roaming the streets, our area was notorious for the number of times it made to the news because of the people who were murdered here and you would hear about a theft every so often. In addition to that, when we were growing up, it was not unusual for us to hear gunshots on a regular basis, which were often preceded or followed by people yelling at each other and fighting with each other.

I think this pretty much gives you an idea that this was definitely not the place where you wanted to raise your family. Most people were reluctant to venture out during the night, let alone during the day.

I am quite certain that you won't be surprised with what I am going to add next. A stereotype that was associated with people from my neighborhood was that if you lived in this region, you probably were not going to get anywhere in life and you were bound to end up gangbanging, in jail, pregnant as a teen or, worse, dead. As you can see, this basically meant that I should pretty much have been doomed for the dumps.

Fast forward several years. I was going to a restaurant in the North End with my co-workers for lunch. As we were driving through the region, one of my co-workers advised us all that it would be better if we closed all our windows and locked the doors because we were driving through the North End now. When she made that comment, I have to admit that I felt pretty ashamed and embarrassed of the fact that I lived in the North End.

I was soon able to overcome my embarrassment though. I stopped giving a fuck about what people thought. What people do not realize is that the incidents that took place in the North End were isolated incidences. These took place between people who had beef against each other. I, too, had lived in this neighborhood for so long and I can vouch for the fact that nothing too bad has ever happened to me. I mean, in a region that is only known for its murderers and drug dealers, having your house broken into is not a pretty big deal, is it now?

And let me just add another thing here. A few paragraphs ago, I mentioned the stereotype that exists for people who live in the North End. Did I end up as part of a gangbang? Did I end up in jail? Did I have to deal with a teenage pregnancy? No. I made it somewhere in life. I am happy with what I have achieved in my life. I am happy at where I stand in life today.

Because of my own background, I am able to better pick out the common theme among my coaches and mentors; the common theme is that all these individuals decided to rise from the ashes and that they all understood that their experiences of hardship, failure and fear have helped to shape them into the successful people they are today. Elizabeth Kubler Ros says, "The most beautiful people we have known are those who have known defeat, known suffering, known struggle, known loss, and have found a way out of the depths. These people have an appreciation, a sensitivity, and an understanding of life that fills them will compassion, gentleness, and a deep loving concern. Beautiful people do not just happen."

When hardship does enter our life along with a continual series of unfortunate events, we do tend to ask for life to take it easy on us. However, having an easy life does not stretch or challenge us. Contrary to what one may think, having a super easy life where things automatically fall into your lap is not the key to growth. This is because we need challenges and we need the drive to overcome those challenges, as this will ultimately allow us to grow more and be more. I also think it is important to point out that the more we become, the more we can give to others. It is through our failures and hardships in life that others look at us and wonder how is it that we are able to cope with the curveballs that life has given us. The skills and abilities we have learned to cope will allow us to help others in need. Also, I think we fail to remember that things happen for a reason and that they are just preparing us for future situations that will try and test our current capabilities. Jim Rohn states, "Don't wish that your life was easier, just wish you were better." Instead of asking that your life becomes easier, ask for life to provide you with the experiences, knowledge, skills and abilities to handle any difficulty you come across. Trust that the experience is molding you into the amazing and successful person you were meant to be. Arnold Schwarzenegger once said: "I like the pain that makes me the champion. The way you deal with pain divides the champion from the rest." I have learned to love the pain that makes me a champion; they say that diamonds are created by extreme amounts of pressure exerted on to them. Know that these negative experiences will pressure you into becoming that diamond. It is now your time to shine.

I've talked quite a bit about inner strength and resilience, as well as my own personal experience. So how do you build up this inner strength? The first step would be to learn to accept who you are. You need to come to terms with your own identity and make peace with it. Two of the biggest obstacles, apart from fear, that you will face in life are regret and guilt as you move along the path towards self-acceptance. However, as we have discussed earlier, you need to learn to forgive yourself and to look at your failures as learning experiences. Reflect back on what happened and the skill or life lesson that it taught you, and you will slowly realize that you have improved as an individual in very tangible ways. Knowing this has helped me in accepting myself and my past.

The second step, which is also equally important, is that you spend time and surround yourself with people who treat you exactly the way you deserve to be treated. You have to recognize the fact that you are a valuable individual and you deserve to be treated exactly that way. This means that sometimes you might have to cut out certain people from your life. At that time, it might seem a little hard; just trust me when I say that you will realize that it was totally worth it in the long run. For example, you can probably think of at least one or more people in your life who only stick around while life is going good. These people are called fair-weather friends. However, when the going gets tough, you will find that these people just appear to be a little too busy to help you out or even to talk to you. You should make yourself strong enough to say no to such people and stay away from them. Instead, you should focus on making friends with people who are always ready to help you out and invest as much as you do (or maybe even more) into the relationship. It is wise to avoid people who are habitually cruel, negative, demanding and selfish. Instead, seek the company of individuals who are respectful, supportive, loving, and creative.

The third step is to build up your self-reliance. There are different things you can do to build self-reliance. For example, think about all you have achieved in life, which will help you realize that there is lots that you are capable of accomplishing.

The fourth step is to try out new things, enjoy them, embrace the small hurdles along the way and learn from them. Yes, hurdles will come eventually and there is no one who can truthfully claim to be perfect. If you think that you have a certain flaw, it is equally possible that someone else sees that as a unique quality and not a flaw.

The fifth step in which you can increase your inner strength is to focus on affirmations. They play a crucial role in increasing your focus and improving your determination, which helps you in delving into the vast reserves of your inner strength. For example, a great way of doing this is to repeat positive phrases right when you wake up in the morning or just before you are ready to go to sleep. These phrases should be used to remind you that you have to believe in yourself and that you are a valuable human being. A lot of people find affirmations to be even more effective when they stand in front of the mirror and repeat them to themselves. For example, a simple phrase like, "I can do this" or "I am destined for greatness" can also take you a long way.

The sixth step is to indulge in your passion and carry out activities that you enjoy. For example, if you find your peace when you have buried your nose deep into a novel, take out time each day (or if that's too much, then every alternate day) for reading. Find yourself a cozy corner to read. Maybe it's your bed or a small little corner tucked away in some part of the house. Get yourself a healthy snack to munch on while you read and put your phone aside so that you will not be disturbed. Spend quality time with yourself. Be grateful for the small little things that you can treat yourself to once in a while. Life can be stressful when you are working, managing household chores, trying to stay within budgets, and also looking after your family at the same time. It can get very tiring and you might find yourself losing some of your inner strength. In order to cut down on your stress, you can find ways of relaxing, such as taking a long warm bath, running a few miles or meditating alone. Once you find a certain activity that can help you relax, you will find it easier to recover from the setbacks of your life. If something troublesome happens, you can simply walk away and indulge in your favorite activity and it is guaranteed to give your mood a boost.

If you are trying to build up your inner strength, you can try to volunteer in your local area. Helping out others is an excellent and very effective way of feeling better about yourself and it also gives you time to reflect on how everyone is suffering in their own way; you are not the only one. Change can be brought about through the help of others. You can do a quick search online to find out if there are any volunteer programs being run in your community. For example, you may want to help out at the local kitchen that provides food to the homeless or you can go to a nursing home to read and mingle with seniors who crave the company of others. Needless to say, engaging in such activities will also help you realize that you are much better off than others and a little clarity from time to time is sure to do you good.

So we come down to this. Life is not easy. You will face challenges. You will struggle. You will fall down. There will be days when you won't feel like getting out of bed. There will be days when you wouldn't want to see your own face in the mirror, but you can use your inner strength to change these challenges into positive learning experiences. You can use a setback as the reason for why you need to do even better in the future or why you need to get out of bed to start working even harder to achieve what you want.

CHAPTER 7 – EXERCISE

Check out www.carolbanayos.com/bonuses to complete the Chapter 7 Exercise for Resilience and Inner Strength.

CHAPTER 8

Breaking out of Conformity and Finding Your Passion and Purpose in Life

"The opposite of courage in our society is not cowardice – It is conformity." Rollo May

Let's start off by reflecting on what a few famous personalities have had to say about conformity. According to Rita Mae Brown, a famous American feminist and writer, "The reward for conformity is that everyone likes you except you yourself." Former United States President, Mr. John F. Kennedy, stated, "Conformity is the jailer of freedom and the enemy of growth." My own mentor and life success coach, Tony Robbins, was quoted to have said that, "In life, choose to be the chess player, rather than the chess piece."

Take a moment to analyze what these people think about conformity. It seems like no one really views it in a positive light. What do you stand to lose if you conform to others or society? Well, according to Rita Brown, chances are that you will not really like the person you have become. Similarly, it seems that John F. Kennedy feels that conforming to the opinion or practices of the masses means that one is no longer free in the truest sense of being free and that their conformity will hinder personal growth and development. Lastly, Tony Robbins sums up what Brown and Kennedy have tried to say in just a few words of advice: it is better to manage one's own affairs and be in charge of them rather than going along with what others are doing or saying.

When I started to become consciously aware of my thoughts and surroundings, I realized that I was stuck in conformity. I was going along with everyone else's flow, instead of trying to manage or direct the flow in the direction that I wanted to move in. Earl Nightingale says, "The number one disease in the world is conformity." For me, it really was a disease that was bringing me down, just like any other physical disease would. For starters, I pursued an education that would provide me with the right background for a career that was safe because of the benefits that it had to offer. For years, I thought my dream would be to go to university and get into Human Resources. A couple of weeks after I graduated from university for my second degree, I started working for the government in the Human Resource department. My university was having a career fair and I remember one of the only places I submitted my resume to was the Province of Manitoba. I got an entry-level position and worked hard to move up to the position of Human Resource Consultant. I really thought that was what I wanted. Looking back now, I can tell that there were certain clues signaling that this was not the job for me.

However, at that time, I did not pay any attention to them. For instance, I was at a retirement party probably two to three years into my position and I remember two of my coworkers were speaking and one of them said to the other, "That's going to be you in the next 25 years!" And he was totally okay with it. I thought to myself at that moment, "That sounds like a 25 to life prison sentence..." I could not imagine working at the same place or let alone working for someone my whole life. I realized that I did all this because I was conditioned from childhood that I needed to go to school, work hard and get a great education so that I could get a job. I was following and behaving in accordance with the socially accepted conventions and standards; most of us operate in that way. We don't listen to ourselves and we let society tell us what we should do. I can bet that more than half of the people reading this will be pausing right about now as a similar memory comes flooding back, where they have acted on something that is based purely on what is acceptable and desirable according to their society.

We are like Alice from Alice in Wonderland when she talks to the cat and asks,

"Would you tell me, please, which way I ought to go from here?"

CAROL BANAYOS

"That depends a good deal on where you want to get to," said the cat.

"I don't much care where," said Alice.

"Then it doesn't much matter which way you go," said the cat

I decided that I was going to break out of conformity by pursuing my dreams and creating the life that I always wanted for myself. I also always had thoughts of being an entrepreneur and took business opportunities with people alongside network marketing. I can now think of a number of reasons why these opportunities did not turn out to be as lucrative for me as I thought they would have been. I understand now that this simply did not resonate with me; I did not get the sense of fulfillment that I should have gotten if I really was doing something that I wanted to do. After I realized this reality, it really hit me that I needed to start thinking for myself. So this is how I started thinking about things that I was genuinely passionate about. What got me excited? What motivated me to work harder or to work more? Two things popped into my mind. The first thing was having my own real estate business, and the second thing was visiting Australia and then touring the rest of the world from there. At this point, I could do either of the two. I chose the latter because this was a dream of sorts that I had harbored since I was in high school. I had always dreamed of going to Australia and travelling all over the world.

I decided to give myself a year to get all my shit in order before I quit my job. There were a number of things that I needed to get done with before I could pursue my plans. Yes, I was going to do what I had wanted to do since forever and what I was passionate about, but I could not just give up everything all of a sudden and leave. The wise thing to do is think everything through. Go with what your heart desires, but a little planning is also required so that you can make sure you actually achieve what you have desired for so long. I had to sell my house and so I had to get started with the necessary renovations to get it on the market. Next, I went to the travel agency to get my work visa for Australia and decided to add on New Zealand. The reason for New Zealand is because I love Lord of the Rings and had to visit the Shire and meet the Hobbits. Several months later, in April of 2013, I went to Australia to activate my work visa. It was an amazing experience and I learned a lot from my short trip.

I was even more excited to get my shit in order and be back in Australia by October 2013. In May 2013, my friend who happened to be a real estate investor and who I bought my first house from told me about a real estate course that was happening in June 2013 and that I should check it out. I took a couple of real estate courses in the past but it didn't really click with me and found that their practices were more of a scheme to get money from people rather than results. The reason why I decided to take this course is because I respected my friend's opinion and the guy who was teaching the course was popular in the field. So, as my friend suggested, I took the real estate course in June 2013 and at the end of the course I was offered a job that would have truly been a dream job. Except, at that time, it was a confusion. How was it a very perfect job for anyone else in my position who wasn't ready to set off on the same quest as me? Well, firstly, they offered me a starting salary that matched my salary at the Province and, in addition to that, the job would also allow me to work from home and make my own hours. Basically, there was additional money and greater flexibility of work hours. I was very confused about what I should do. Yes, at one point I had thought about the real estate market, but now I had been planning for well over a year to go to Australia. I had already sold my house and activated my visa. At this point, I had to pause what I was doing and force myself to weigh the pros and cons of my current situation. After thoroughly reviewing everything, I decided to take the job offer because it would allow me to gain the experience that I would need to start my own real estate business in the future; at the same time, it also offered me the flexibility to travel all over the world at any time I wanted.

In June 2013, I quit my job as a Human Resource Consultant and started my new job with the real estate company in August, just over one month later. I am happy that I took the risk of pursuing my passion because I have no regrets of whether I should have done something else or could have done something else. Also, I now got the feeling that I was following the beat of my own drum and that I was choosing the direction that I wanted my life to take. I was creating my own trail; instead of blindly following the path that had been frequently trodden by others or that had been paved out by other people, I was trailblazing, which was something that I was feeling pretty good about.

I feel that the greatest success that one could have would be to be able to live life in his or her own way. In order to do this, it is important for you to know that you can't be someone else's puppet. You will see a lot of people around you conforming to societal conventions and doing what others are asking them to do. You will also be caught up in the same thing. You will sometimes give in to doing what your family tells you to do, whereas at other times you will find yourself acting in the same way as those around you, regardless of whether or not you truly believe in that action yourself. You need to remember that the ultimate choice is always just your own and that only you have the right and the power to make your own decisions.

A powerful quote I once heard was, "Be true to yourself or you aren't true to anyone." For some reason, this resonates very strongly with me. If you ever tell someone else a lie, you will be likely to get away with it. I mean, yes, there is a chance that you might be caught, but sooner or later the other person will forget and you will be more than happy to do the same. However, it is not quite the same when you lie to yourself. A fundamental problem in today's world is that people spend so much time focusing on what those around them are doing or what society demands of them or what the ideal life or status should be according to the standards set by others. In doing so, they forget what their own heart is trying to whisper to them. All I would like to say is this: failure is inevitable. Yes, you might feel you are doing pretty well in the short run, but in the longer run, if you suddenly think that you spent your entire life living a hollow, meaningless life and failed to achieve anything that you desired yourself, then you can't really call yourself successful, can you?

Sometimes you will find yourself working extra hard to please others; there is no harm in doing that. Make others happy, especially if their happiness means a lot to you. Work hard to make your parents proud and be good to your spouse and be the best parent you can be for your children. However, in making others happy, it is important for us to remember that it would not be wise for us to let go of what our own values are or what we truly want from life. You do not want to be the person who constantly realigns his or her values to suit those of others and ends up with no stance or values of their own.

In creating your own path and paving your way down it, you will also have to leave the comfort provided by your nest. At times, you will not even realize the kind of vicious rut you have been sucked into, where you do the same thing again and again and again. As has been said in the great dictator's speech in Charlie Chaplin, we merely become machine men with machine hearts and machine minds. But is that who we want to be? Will that lead to the place we are destined to be? I don't think so. You cannot possibly expect yourself to grow and progress and develop as an individual or as a professional if you continue doing the same thing every single day of the year. You should not simply be existing; you should try to live a little, for which you will have to leave the comfort that routines offer to people. Sometimes you will have to navigate your way through uncharted territory and violent waters, but remember that it is these tumultuous waters and rocky terrain that will lead you to the shore and summit of your goals.

To leave the comfort of the daily rut of life, one has to make choices. This can be a daunting task in itself. How do you know you are doing the right thing? What if your plan fails? What if you let go of a better option for something that was destined for failure right from the start? Still, if you never take the risk, how will you know that you made the right decision? One should always try hard to overcome the natural fears nestled deep inside and listen to their heart instead. If you can't get yourself to make your own decisions, then do not even try thinking about getting to your goals. I am sorry to burst your bubble, but it will not happen.

CAROL BANAYOS

It is not that easy. It never was and never will be. Stop caring about what others think and stop thinking about what others are going to say to you. You have the right to express your own passions and pursue them to any degree that you want. You should be the one telling others how you want to live your life instead of having others tell you how you should be living yours.

Ralph Marston has a poem on your living purpose: "Your purpose is not to fear or to frighten. Your purpose is not to control or be controlled. Your purpose is to live, love and to experience life in a way that is uniquely yours. Your purpose is to be open to the newness and reality of every moment, giving joy a living expression. Your purpose is to give the miracle of life a distinct voice. It is to know and to treasure moments of pure beauty for which there are no words. The challenges may be profound, and yet they cannot challenge or diminish your purpose. On the contrary, those challenges help you to understand and express your purpose more clearly. The world, at times, distracts you into caring about mere shadows of life that have no real meaning. Yet always, beneath the surface, your living purpose is there. Remember that purpose, and let its value flow freely from you with each thought, feeling and action. Live from your purpose and be fully alive." This has led me to discover my own purpose. I have now found a way in which I can help my family and friends and create a better life for myself. In this way, I hope to have a positive impact on the lives of others and to inspire them to follow their own path.

Remember, this is your life and you are the only one living it. No two people tread on the same path as each other and everyone faces their own inner demons and struggles. From time to time, your path may overlap with those of others but, at the end of the day, it will only be you. Although there might be people along the way who can guide you and steer you towards the right direction, remember that ultimately everyone walks down that path on their own. In light of this, it is important for everyone to remember to follow their own instincts, stay true to oneself and listen to what their heart says.

As the great William Shakespeare says, "To thine own self be true."

And this I shall do.

CHAPTER 8 – EXERCISE

Check out www.carolbanayos.com/bonuses to complete the Chapter 8 Exercise for Breaking out of Conformity and Finding Your Passion and Purpose in Life.

CHAPTER 9

Be Your Authentic Self

"The authentic self is the soul made visible."
Sarah Ban Breathnach

Sarah Ban Breathnach sums up the authentic self perfectly. I found that once I broke out of conformity I started to begin to express myself from my absolute core that was fully encompassing all my uniqueness. My uniqueness stemmed from my beliefs, skills, ability, and experiences rather than the role and function I had in society.

When I think of who I am, I think of myself as a spiritual being made up of source energy that is constantly changing and evolving based on the experience I choose to have for myself.

To become your authentic self all you need to do is look within. When you are following your intuition, which I like to call your inner compass, along with following your true passion in life you can begin the journey to your authentic self. And when you look within, you will find true love, kindness, and compassion.

Ben Okri says, "The most authentic thing about us is our capacity to create, to overcome, to endure, to transform, to love and be greater than our suffering."

However, most people operate from the false self. What is a false self? A false self is sort of like an idealized character you have in your mind and based on that, you attempt to project an artificial persona. This can be done for a number of reasons. For example, some people might not feel confident enough to express what they truly think or what they believe in. They lack confidence to the extent that they even doubt their own opinions and their own beliefs if they are not in accordance with those held by the majority.

In order to understand that, let's take a look at this very simple example. Let's suppose I have a green card in my hand and I show it to a group of fifty people. These fifty people tell me that the card is pink, which is incorrect. When I show the card to you, what will your answer be? Will you tell me it is green because you know it is green, knowing that that might incite insult or abuses from the others and also knowing that it will make you stand apart from the rest? Or will you tell me that the card is pink, because after seeing fifty people tell me that the card is pink, you are beginning to doubt whether you identified the color correctly in the first place?

This might seem like a very silly example, but think over it and try to apply it to bigger situations and you will soon come to realize how much we tend to conform to what society and the people around us have predetermined for us. Sometimes we just find it easier to say what others are saying, to adhere to the same beliefs as them, to take on the values that they hold close to them and basically, to become clones of each other. This just eliminates the process of having to explain to someone why you are different from them or why you are not ascribing to the same values as them. And this tends to happen across ages, across cultures and across races.

Once you realize that you are in conformity and break free from it and the social norms, you can then follow your passion and express yourself from your absolute core. This may seem scary for you since most people are scared that who they really are is not good enough. So they act from their false self that is a role or function from which others expect them to act. We tend to follow the expectations of others or the standards they have set for us, be that society, your family, and your friends. And for the majority of people it maybe easier to operate as your false self because it's how you have been operating your whole life.

Functioning from the false self is never fulfilling and you will feel a sense of emptiness and void to be filled and you won't know why you are always having those feelings. Along with feeling emptiness you can also feel exhausted. Why? Because it is draining to continually act like someone else just to be liked. It takes up a good deal of energy when you are trying to put up a façade or when you are trying to be someone you are not because it does not come naturally to you. You have to make an effort to ensure that you align yourself with the demands, expectations and standards of others around you. It's like that song, The Great Pretender by The Platters. However, I think one of the most harmful things that happens when you act from the false self is that it diminishes the soul and buries your true greatness.

There is nothing to gain but everything to lose when you are operating from your false self. We are all such beautiful multifaceted beings who should be embracing our uniqueness and owning it. Why act like someone else, that role is already taken by them. Be your true authentic self.

Oprah Winfrey says, "I had no idea that being your authentic self could make me as rich as I've become. If I had, I'd have done it a lot earlier." And you all know where Oprah Winfrey's attempt at being her own true self has taken her, right? So maybe it is time for us all to take a leaf out of her book as well. You will be surprised at how far it can take you, perhaps not in worldly terms, but let me tell you that it will put you at ease. It will help you achieve that oneness with yourself that we previously talked about. It will make it easier for you to get to the place that you are destined to be simply because now you will be aware of what you want from life and how you want to go about it. It sounds so easy, right, when someone says, "learn to embrace yourself." It is not so easy. Sometimes our fears and insecurities get the best of us. But life will be a blessing when you eventually learn to do that. So do not put this off until you are old and you see your life ending. If you are reading this now and even if you are only twenty years old, learn from the personal experiences that I have been telling you about.

CHAPTER 9 – EXERCISE

Check out www.carolbanayos.com/bonuses to complete the Chapter 9 Exercise for Be Your Authentic Self.

CHAPTER 10

Making Assumptions Causes Drama

"Making assumptions simply means believing things are a certain way with little or no evidence that shows you are correct, and you can see at once how this can lead to terrible trouble." Lemony Snicket

Don Miquel Ruiz is quoted to have said, "Don't make assumptions. Find the courage to ask questions and to express what you really want. Communicate with others as clearly as you can to avoid misunderstandings, sadness, and drama. With just this one agreement, you can completely transform your life."

One of my mentors gave me a book to read, which was called The Four Agreements by Don Miquel Ruiz. I love this book because it puts many things into perspective, especially how we all tend to make assumptions.

Don Miquel Ruiz says, "We make the assumption that everyone sees life the way we do. We assume that others think the way we think, feel the way we feel, judge the way we judge, and abuse the way we abuse. This is the biggest assumption that humans make. And this is why we fear being ourselves around others. Because we think everyone else will judge us, victimize us, abuse us, and blame us as we do ourselves. So even before others have a chance to reject us, we have already rejected ourselves. That is the way the human mind works."

This new perspective on my assumptions made me do something I thought I would never be capable of doing. Here is what happened. My ex, who also happens to be my first love came back into my life and I tried to avoid any interactions with him for the longest time. However, since I was not in a relationship and it was about ten years since we were together, I thought, what the hell, what is the worse that can happen right? Well since I never gave myself the time to get over him when I broke it off, it hit me like lightning that I was still in love with him. He was always in the back of my mind and I constantly wondered how it would be if we ever got back together. I know it seems stupid especially since he lied and cheated when we were together. Sometime love is blind and it makes you do irrational and do stupid shit. Also, people do change. I tried so hard to avoid him and turn off what I was feeling but the more I resisted, the more it persisted.

Benjamin Disraeli says, "The magic of our first love is our ignorance that it will never end." I decided to follow my heart rather than my mind and tell him how I felt. My reasoning was that I never want to look back at my life and regret that I should have said or did something. And I knew I faced rejection but I was okay with that, I just needed to get it off my chest and deal with it.

So this is exactly what I did and what I said to my ex. I asked him out for coffee and said, "There is a reason why I asked to meet with you and the reason is that I have to tell you something and there is no easy way of saying it so here goes. I am still in love with you. And I love everything about you and would not change one thing. You have this greatness, your resourceful, and have this mind quality that I can appreciate. I told him I have no expectation of any outcomes from me telling him this. This was weighing real heavy on my heart and had to tell you. You have always been in the back of my mind and I did not want to have any regrets by not telling you. "

As the great Wallace Wattles says, "An ounce of doing is worth more than a pound of theorizing." After I told him that, I got up ready to leave and he said, "you can't just leave after telling me something like that." It definitely took him off guard. He said, "that he thought that was never an option considering what he did to me and that he always tried to recreate what we had with the people he has been with." We spent the next several hours talking and I asked questions I have always wanted to ask him but was too scared, like why he cheated and he said, "He sincerely felt alone and had issues and went about dealing with them the wrong way."

At that moment, I realized that the majority of our fights were due to me feeling insecure and worthless because I did not address the feelings I had about him cheating and lying earlier on in the relationship and it just made me act crazy. And I think it would cause any girl to act this way. It is not easy when you love someone as hard as I did tell you that he is not cheating when you know that he is. It is like putting a band-aid over an open wound. It just won't ever heal itself. There were times when I could have cheated several times but I would not be able to look myself in the mirror if I had gone through with it.

We made plans to see each other again, hugged, and we went our ways. Needless to say, that was the last time we ever saw and spoke to each other again. There was a poem I wrote for him when we were together and it ended something like this.

We are like a book with no table of contents each chapter unfolding to a new level of bliss. There is no way of knowing how the story will end but fate is how the story begun. Well, I can now say I know how that story has ended. You may be thinking I am crazy for doing this and making myself vulnerable to rejection and pain. The reality is I would be causing myself more pain by holding this in and wondering what if.

And no matter what I have been through with my exes, I still wish them the best in love and life. Also, what is more important is that I will never stop being a romantic at heart. I know these experiences are preparing me for my true love, my twin flame. And it will be all worth it in the end.

CHAPTER 10 – EXERCISE

Check out www.carolbanayos.com/bonuses to complete the Chapter 10 Exercise for Making Assumptions Causes Drama.

CHAPTER 11

Struggle and Pain is Inevitable. Belief Is King

"Some of our struggle involve making decisions, while others are a result of the decision we have made. Some of our struggles result from choices others make that affect our lives. We cannot always control everything that happens to us in this life, but we can control how we respond. Many struggles come as problems and pressures that sometime cause pain. Others come as temptations, trials, and tribulations." L. Lionel Kendrick

"Back your belief with a resolute will and you will become unconquerable, a master of men among men....yourself." Claude Bristol

As I mentioned in an earlier chapter, in June 2013, I quit my Human Resource Consultant Job and in August 2013 started my new job with the real estate company. It was a new position and I was in charge of creating and developing it. I was really confident that I would succeed.

However, it so turned out that the job was difficult and challenging. Not only did I fail try after try but I also came across some really dishonest people, which hurt me, because you always try to think the best of people and I thought most people were like that. Man, did I have a rude awakening. I guess it was another one of those moments where I suddenly had to wake the fuck up.

One day as I was heading off to breakfast right before meeting my client, I got a call from my boss. He asked if I was okay and I said. "I was perfectly fine." He said, "the police came to the office looking for you." I said. "what the hell, why would they come to the office?" So I tried calling my family too see if everything was okay with them. I then get a call from the police asking me to come home because they need to speak to me. I get back home and there are cops everywhere and they have just raided my place. Before I know it I was hand cuffed and placed in the back of the cop car. I was so confused and didn't know what was going on. The cop was speaking to me as I was in the back seat of the cop car, asking me if I am aware of what I was being charged with and I said I don't know what you are talking about. I was in shock.

I get placed into a room where the detectives start questioning me. I am still in shock and zoned out and was staring at the corner of the room. When reality started kicking in, I let out some tears and was advised by legal aid to say I cannot not comment or have nothing to say.

I am not sure how long I was in that room but it felt like forever. I was then brought down stairs to get my fingerprints and pictures taken, then I was taken down stairs to get checked again. I ran into my friend's husband who is a correctional officer there. I was so embarrassed. He had to ask me questions and he was trying to console me. After that I was placed in another concrete room. I was then handcuffed again and placed in the back of a van and brought to this building where I was placed in a room with two female officers. They told me to strip and bend over and cough. I was so humiliated and felt like my privacy was violated. My clothes were taken away and I was told to take a shower.

At this point I was like, what the fuck I'm not going home? Nope! I take a shower and I have to wear these white, used, blood stained granny panties, sports bras, gray shirt, and large gray pants with a yellow strip down each leg. Of course, these clothes were washed but I was so fucking disgusted that I had to wear these underwear and clothes. I was then placed in another concrete room with three bunk beds and one stainless steel toilet. This room was the hole. I was in this room for three to four days. This time period was absolutely horrible. There was no way of knowing what time it was and it was cold as fuck in there. I asked for another blanket and sweater and was denied. I also asked to take a shower, and that too, was denied. So not only do I have to stay in this hole, I also have to use the washroom in front of these strangers.

To top it off I was starving. I did not eat meat or drink milk and all the meals came with meat and milk. There was barely any fruit and veggies. I really thought I was stuck in a mental psych ward or in some horrible nightmare I would soon wake up from. I kept on wondering when the fuck I would get out of here. I had some visitors. I was brought up stairs and was placed in another room.

I met with legal aid and of course I was not approved for that because of my salary. Another lawyer came and I asked them to get me the fuck out of here as soon as possible. My family came to visit me and as soon as I saw my parents and sisters I started crying profusely. I told them I needed to get out of here. This place is going to make me go crazy.

I was then transferred with all the other inmates and now in jail. I didn't know how long I might be in jail for so I asked to see the nurse so I can talk to them about my dietary needs. I told him that I do not eat meat or dairy and asked if I could get vegan meals. He told me no, and that I would have to be Muslim. I said, "Well I am Muslim now." Needless to say, I was denied. So I had to resort to trading my milk and meat dishes with other inmates for fruits and veggies. It was so sad. I also learned how to make tweezers since they didn't sell any in concession. I learnt that when the other inmates got their Ritz individual cracker with spreadable cheese, they could use the plastic to spread the cheese as tweezers by bending it in half. I tried it and it worked really well.

We all had to go to bed by 10pm and be awake by 7am. We were not allowed to leave our bunks only if we were to use the washroom. Failure to follow the rules, you would be placed in the hole again. God knows I didn't want to go back there again. We all had chores to do. I had to clean the washrooms, sweep, mop, and dust. I played games with the other girls that I never played before such as clue and charades. It was a nice escape. I noticed right after we were done the games we fell into this slumber state because reality started to settle in that we were still in this hellhole.

Days went by so slow and I tried to read to pass the time but it was difficult to focus. One of the inmates told me that the girl sleeping in my bottom bunk axed someone in the head. I was freaking out but then I thought she was just probably bullshitting and said that to try to scare me. The next morning we were having breakfast and she came to sit with me. I decided to ask her why she was in here. She said, "I axed someone in the head but was more of a love tap." I was going to get up and leave but I didn't want to be her next victim.

Later that day in the evening, that same girl was teasing some of the other girls to come and sit on her face. Yes, she was a lesbian. Not that there is anything wrong with that. She then started harassing me and I yelled out, "I only like DICK." She replied, "Oh, I'm going to need a bottle of water for you cause you're spicy. "

The next day, I was happy to learn that my family put some money in my canteen. I was finally able to get some food, chap stick, real toothpaste, toothbrush, shampoo, conditioner, and lotion. Some of the inmates that were arrested didn't have any money in their canteen yet so I got them some items. I was forced to use what was available, which was these small packets of shampoo and soap that made your hair disgusting and the soap made your skin so dry and scaly. And no, I didn't have any lotion. The toothpaste was gross and the toothbrush was so flimsy that it didn't do the job. I felt like things were looking up. It felt like Christmas when my stuff came in. The excitement made me want to shower and make myself comfortable.

There were talks about the news that evening and that they were going to show my name. I was horrified. I watched the news and I was happy no pictures were shown of me nor was my name mentioned.

But that didn't last long. My name did end up appearing in the news and online. I was so mortified and embarrassed. I know you shouldn't care about what people think but this was not some small-scale issue or incident this was a large-scale character assassination against me. The news and media painted me to be this criminal, knowing fully well what I was getting into and doing. To be honest, I was hurt that people can be so mean and cruel.

Another thing that made this even worse for me is that I used to work for the Provincial Government in Human Resources and I am sure they all know. I am sure everyone knows and will judge me. The same thing kept on repeating in my mind: what will they think about me? Will they ever give me the same respect that they once gave me? Will they look at me with the same eyes?

At this moment, reality started to sink in and the possibility that I may be charged for crimes that I did not commit and serve a lengthy sentence. All these thoughts were going through my head. This could not be happening to me. I have so much I need to do and accomplish. I could not fathom the thought of missing life by being in jail, waiting away and not fulfilling my full potential. This by far was the most horrific experience I have ever been through. Over a week had passed and my Lawyer informed me that I was getting released. But I would have various conditions such as; a curfew where I had to remain within my residence from 9pm to 6am, I could not leave Manitoba, talk to certain people, carry any weapons (like I had any), and a bunch of other crap. At that point in time I didn't care what it said, I just wanted out. I was so fucking excited to get out. The first thing I wanted to do was go and eat a delicious meal. So I did and it was so satisfying and tasted amazing. I had rice with deep fried battered eggplant, vegetables, and eggrolls.

The day that I got out, was the day that I had a cooking class that I signed up for. I could not attend because it was going to run past my curfew. When I got home I was really emotional and started crying. I asked GOD what I did to deserve this. It just seemed that my whole existence was filled with continuous hardship, struggle, pain, and failure. And yes I did fall into the victim mode of why me. The next day, I had to call my boss. He figured out that I got arrested and was very understanding and did not fire me. I was very grateful and asked if I could use two weeks of my vacation time to get my shit in order by getting my mind right and clean up the tornado of a mess the police left behind when they raided the condo I was staying in. That day I decided that I would only give myself these two weeks to deal and grieve with what happened to me and move forward.

Someone told me about Orange Is The New Black. I resonated with this show and it brought to me some new realizations and added some humor to my situation. Next thing I did was to clean up my condo. It literally took me three full days to clean it up. When that was done, I knew I had to get in contact with some of the people I was working with and to my surprise some of them cut me off and I never heard from them. I guess they didn't want the negative press they may receive by working with me. That hurt because I didn't expect that from this person. I also had to get in touch with my best friends. I am so grateful because they were there for me and didn't judge me at all. They were worried about me since I didn't contact them right away. Some of my friends didn't actually know about it and was informed by someone in Japan and in the United States. I couldn't believe it reached that far. My family and friends said to look online to what was being said about me. Five pages filled with coverage. I was told in prison about it but it's another thing to read about yourself and being painted as this fucking criminal. I was deflated and knew I could not put myself in victim mode because that person the media was making me out to be wasn't me. I had to become a victor of my circumstance and knew I needed to listen to Tony Robbin's Ultimate Edge Program again to get me in check.

I was assigned to a probation officer. I was happy that he was nice and seemed very empathic. Since I was working from home and making my own hours, I had to call him every morning to tell him what I was doing, where I was going and when. Two weeks later, I'm back at work, getting back into the groove of things. It seemed that everything was going great in real estate. Things soon began to down spiral. I was working on a couple of deals and the clients went MIA, the broker who I was using at the time was stealing my clients, and was just running into one unfortunate situation one after the other. I really started to hate what I was doing. I was working sometimes seventeen hours days and no results to show for it. I was getting down on myself. I quit my permanent Human Resource Consultant position with the Province that I worked so hard to achieve to follow my passion in real estate where it has just been one failure after the other. I didn't understand and was embarrassed. About three months later, my boss met with me and said he had to let me go. I definitely understood where he was coming from. But at that moment, I was the happiest I've been in a long time.

I knew I had to move out of the condo I was renting because I could no longer afford it. I had to move back in with my parents. I felt like I was taking so many steps back in my life. At my age I really thought I would have all my shit together, going through this shit was that last thing I could ever imagine.

I realized that possibly the reason why I continued to fail was that I was not meant to work for anyone and fulfill their dreams and that I had to go on my own and create it. Another thing I realized is that I didn't ask for help where I should have. I wanted to control all the variables to ensure things were done right not realizing that I should have delegated some of my tasks, so I could be more efficient on the bigger picture items. I realized that real estate is not an easy thing and that there are snakes and shady people out there. I knew if this was something that I was going to continue doing, I would need to guard my emotions by not feeling sad about the people that try to hurt me and know that those type of people exist out there. I vowed to myself that I would only work with people with whom I trust and seek help when I need it.

So now I am unemployed and living back home with my parents. I had to apply for Employment Insurance, which I thought I would never have to do. I thought I could apply for another job but I couldn't fathom the thought of having to work for someone else. Also, the information in the media about me would deter me from getting a job. Potential employers could just look online and say this chick is a criminal and not hire me. If this wasn't bad enough I got letters from my banks stating that they need to discontinue our banking relationships. Again, I felt like shit. Here I was going to the bank and very friendly with the staff and management. Then this stuff happens and I look like a fraud and criminal. Next, I get a letter from my landlord for the condo saying that she is taking me to court for her door that was damaged by the police for the raid and for the house not being cleaned when I moved out. I did fix the door as well as hired a cleaning company clean the place before I moved out. On top of that I get a letter stating that there is a lien on my car for unpaid parking tickets and that my car can get repossessed at any time. At this point I am laughing. There is a saying that bad luck runs in threes. I call total bullshit on that because this shit was raining on me non-stop. It's more like, when it rains, it pours. "He said that life boils down to standing in line to get shit dropped on your head. Everyone's got a place in the queue, you can't get out of it, and just when you start to congratulate yourself on surviving your dose of shit, you discover that line is actually circular." Scott Lynch, The Republic of Thieves

It's summer and I have to remain within my residence, I can't step my foot outside the front door or be in my yard. The simple pleasures that I enjoy the most such as travelling and camping are not an option because of my curfew and condition to remain within Manitoba. I can't even stay out pass 9pm. Is this really my life right now? In addition, I have to deal with random checks from police officers at my place. I had these ignorant cops pull me over and made rude comments and remarks. They treated me as a criminal. I fucking hated this shit. And when I got home cops came to my place to check on me again. How stupid do these cops think I am to violate any of my conditions? If I violated any of my conditions, I would have to go back to jail and pay $100,000. Jail was horrific. I would never want to go back there again. I really had to start making some fun out of this shit. The last time I was checked on, nine cops, yes nine cops showed up at my parent's house. They checked my room and asked if I had any stacks of cash or drugs laying around. I was shocked at the comment and said of course not.

They looked through all my belongings. I told them if I knew they were coming I would have tidy up a bit for them. I also thanked them for visiting me and told them that is the most action I had in a long time. They all laughed. I just thought what a waste of resources. Nine cops to check on little old me. I guess they need too since I am so dangerous.

I'm 33 years old, unemployed, out on bail, pending charges with numerous things, have a curfew, can't leave Manitoba, and living back at my parents' house. If this isn't enough to make you believe that my situation is as devastatingly real as it gets, I don't know what is. I also have to pay for a Lawyer with my Employment Insurance Wages, which is way less than half of my regular salary. Interesting, isn't it?

However, as rare as it sounds, this is the first time I have been able to feel some sense of freedom. Usually, I am at work or at school. It was hard to get adjusted to not working or keeping busy. Yet, this is exactly what I needed. I needed time to figure out what I wanted to do in life, something that is fulfilling. But now, I had to learn how to relax and be okay with not being busy. I made use of my time by reading a lot, listening to audio programs and videos. Meditation really helped with calming me down and reducing all the noise in my mind. Joined some Meetups in Spirituality along with a Vegan one. During a period of several months I noticed I was doing about six hours of personal development each day. I implemented a morning ritual that I follow each day to ensure I started my day off for success. There are some days that I may miss a meditation session but I always try to be consistent and get right back into my routine. I believe it is important to have a morning ritual in place because not only does it set your day up for success, it also sets the tone. Whenever I have done my morning ritual and something negative or bad happens, I am able to brush it off, and say this too shall pass. Don't get me wrong, I still get pissed and angry sometimes but I don't stay in those states for a long period because those negative feelings don't serve me. It will just bring down a negative spiral and with everything going on, it's the last thing I need to add on my plate. Time does fly by in a blink of an eye. Before I knew it, a year and a half has passed. Nothing has changed in regards to my case.

There were a couple of very upsetting incidents that occurred. One, my case was supposed to have a preliminary trial to where I would have most likely been released as a result of the entire situation. This preliminary trial was cancelled because it was moving straight to trial and from Provincial to Federal Queen's Bench. My Lawyer had to drop me because I didn't have $20,000 and was forced to seek legal aid which I was now approved for since I was unemployed.

I had to come to terms with my situation and make the decision to not care that people were going to judge me or think negatively of me. I knew the truth and that's all that matters. How I made sense out of it was through two things. First, the law of cause and effect and second, that bad things happen to seemly good people.

I know things are meant to happen for a reason but I don't know if I can wrap my mind around this. But at the end of the day, what choice do I have but to accept it. Accept it for what it is. I just tell myself that something better than I could have ever imagined is going to happen and this in a way is preparing me for that amazing journey or opportunity. It was this belief that kept me going. Usually what people believe is a blueprint to the society they create because belief precedes knowledge. As we live and learn about our surroundings in filter, we shape facts to fit our preexisting set of beliefs. Having faith and believing that everything happens for a reason encouraged me to go on to try and find the meaning of what I set out to do in life. It made me realize that belief is irrational, as few of us examine it critically. We simply accept the teachings of our mentors without truly accepting the responsibility that belief entails. We should be accountable for our own convictions and stop accepting ideas blindly.

Paulo Coelho says, "Life has many ways of testing a person's will, either by having nothing happen at all or by having everything happen all at once." And from one of my favorite books by Paulo Coelho, The Alchemist "My heart is afraid that it will have to suffer," Said the boy. "Tell your heart that the fear of suffering is worse than the suffering itself, and no heart has ever suffered when it goes in search of its dreams," Replied the Alchemist.

To be honest, if I did not take the action several years back to personally develop my mental and emotional muscles, I don't think I could have survived this. That was not a pleasant position to be in. Hell, "Not a pleasant position." Does not even serve justice to the torture that I had to go through. It was pure fucking torture. To this day, I do not know how I survived my time there. At times, those days seem entirely unbelievable and I wonder how I lived. I was mentally affected to such an extent that I may have had to be put in a hole, not the one in prison but the one in the psych ward.

I can't stress enough on how important personal development is for an individual, and how impactful a strong belief in oneself can turn out to be. And that the best investment a person can make is to invest in themselves through ways of personal development. With all this shit happening, I still made it a practice to personally develop myself each day by learning, reading, listening to audios, meditation, and working on my goals. This really has made all the difference by keeping me busy and sane. Despite what I was going through, I did not lose sight of where I had to be in life and what I had to achieve for myself. It is good to point out that no matter what is going on in the life that you still have your eyes on the prize and take action each day to work towards your goals no matter what. Also, the saying that, "Time heals all wounds." Is bullshit. It is what you do during that time that heals.

CHAPTER 11 – EXERCISE

Check out www.carolbanayos.com/bonuses to complete the Chapter 11 Exercise for Struggle and Pain is Inevitable. Belief is King.

CHAPTER 12

Conquer Your Fears and Build the Right Type of Confidence

"Do the thing you fear, and continue to do so. This is the quickest and surest way of all victory over fear."
Dale Carnegie

"It we feel secure in the depth of our heart, We shall not challenge anybody, For inner confidence is nothing short of Complete satisfaction." Sri Chinmoy

I see fear in two ways. Firstly, fear is a horrible monster. The more you feed that monster with your thoughts and feelings of fear, the bigger that monster gets. And the bigger the monster gets the more negative impacts it will cause you in a way of procrastination and paralyzing you to act. You convince yourself that the fear of failure is more painful than it is to act. Therefore, fear paralyzes you to the extent of not enabling you to go forth and act on your own will. Secondly, I see it as a way to stretch and grow yourself in a way you never thought possible. To stretch and grow you need to face fear head on by taking action right away towards that goal or situation causing you that fear. It is imperative that you chose the latter, especially if you want to conquer fear, rather than letting it enslave you.

Zig Ziglar says, "F-E-A-R has two meanings: 'Forget Everything And Run' or 'Face Everything And Rise.' This choice is yours."

When I was character assassinated from the media regarding my arrest and the charges, it caused me to be fearful of what others would say or how they would judge me. Also, it caused me to feel ashamed and embarrassed. I was fearful that no one would want to work with me because they would see me as this criminal and not the innocent person I really was. I recognized that feelings of fear and embarrassment only held me back, and this gave me strength, which prevented me from pitying myself. So I faced my fear head on by just being open and honest about what happened to me. I knew I could be faced with rejection and shame, but I knew if they judged me then they were not the right people to work with or be friends with. To my surprise, I was embraced with open arms. Rather than judgment and embarrassment, I was met with courage, bravery, and strength. It is not easy to divulge that kind of information about yourself because you are making yourself vulnerable. But I find if you are honest there is nothing but good that can come out from it. Being open and honest was the best decision I made because rather than making assumptions about how people would react, I killed those assumptions by finding the truth. And as I mentioned in the previous chapter, making assumptions causes drama in your mind and in your life.

What is amazing about conquering your fears is that it helps you build the right type of confidence. And the right type of confidence is inner confidence. When you attack your fears head on it provides you with this sense of confidence on how you approach the goals or situations in life. When you succeed at something, conquering fear can be used as a reference point to remind you of how you overcame your struggles. This can then be applied to the situations in which you lack confidence or strength to go on to remind yourself of how you once conquered what you were afraid of. Inner confidence is not to be confused with external confidence, which is made up from your physical appearances, your job, your status, your lifestyle, your partner, material possessions, wealth, or your perceived confidence. I am not saying that you should not strive for external confidence as it does enhance your overall confidence. What I am saying is that inner confidence is more important and should be the focal point. The reason why I say that inner confidence is more important is because when you lose all your external possession as mention above, the one thing that can't be taken away from you is your inner confidence. That inner confidence will allow you to get back on your feet to start grinding again to recreate or redefined your life. It is with inner confidence that we develop this come back power that would not be apparent to those who only define themselves with their external confidence and possessions.

When people lose everything, they feel that they are a nobody and are powerless. Therefore, they are nothing without their possessions because they defined their entire existence based on what they had, which I think is very dangerous and toxic mindset to have. I have seen it many times when people lose all their possessions, they become depressed, turn to drugs, alcohol, and to the extreme, commit suicide. I truly believe I would have become one of those people if I didn't develop my inner confidence. I pretty much lost everything and now rebuilding and recreating myself. The best way to build inner confidence is to first wake the fuck up and start believing who you are and take the steps to keep building that muscle. The step towards building that muscle is what I indicated in each chapter and throughout this whole book. Such as: be consciously aware; personally grow and develop yourself; learn forgiveness, self-love, acceptance, and self-respect; work on becoming healthy; build resilience and inner strength; become your authentic self.

CHAPTER 12 – EXERCISE

Check out www.carolbanayos.com/bonuses to complete the Chapter 12 Exercise for Conquer your Fears and Build the Right Type of Confidence.

CHAPTER 13

You Are a Magnet

"You are a living magnet, drawing to yourself the people, the resources, and the ideas you need to fulfill what you expect. To the successful it is out of their faith, for others it is out of their fears. If you don't like what you attract, don't change what is coming towards you, change the magnet that is bringing those into your life."
Scot Thomas Anderson

Since I tried very hard to not let what happen to me define who I was and rather focus on my goals in life, I started attracting the right people into my life. The very people I needed and prayed for.

It's an amazing feeling to interact with people with the same mindset. And the ability to voice your thoughts along with collaborate with each other. I come to realize in attaining your goals or any type of success, it is better to do it with a team rather than on your own. I find that since I have attracted these amazing people into my life, it has really propelled me in achieving my goals faster than I expected. And it really has to do with the accountability and playing a bigger game than what you would normally be used to. It's about getting out of your comfort zone. And we all know that saying that life only truly begins at the end of your comfort zone. Claude Bristol says, "With concentrated thought, expectancy, and steadfast belief, we actually set in motion vibratory forces that bring about material manifestation."

When you are surrounded with people who play a bigger game, you naturally want to gravitate to that level. Just like the saying goes, "Birds of the same feather flock together." It has been said, "That you are the average of the five people you spend the most time with." Isn't that reason enough for you to pick up on their habits? Success is either built on the company of good, thoughtful people, or the avoidance of those who bring out the worst in you. Your vibe attracts your tribe, but it also shapes you, and those around you immensely. And for the first time in long time, I can see what I have been envisioned finally coming into fruition. Things are unfolding in ways I could not imagine. Paulo Coelho says, "When you're on a journey to fulfill your personal legend, the whole universe conspires to help you to achieve it."

Despite all the hardship I have been through, I am happy I took risks. You need to take risks in order to go after what you want. And maybe that means you have to quit your job that you are comfortable with to pursue your dreams or move to a different country. Whatever it maybe, life is way to fucking short to be stuck doing something you absolutely hate or something that does not challenge you. When you are given an opportunity to chose between two different roads, choose the one that is less travelled and the one which gives you that feeling in your stomach, a feeling of anticipation and excitement. The poem below is by Robert Frost, which I absolutely love.

Two roads diverged in a yellow wood,
And sorry I could not travel both
And be one traveler, long I stood
And looked down one as far as I could
To where it bent in the undergrowth;

Then took the other, as just as fair,
And having perhaps the better claim
Because it was grassy and wanted wear,
Though as for that the passing there
Had worn them really about the same,

And both that morning equally lay
In leaves no step had trodden black.
Oh, I kept the first for another day!
Yet knowing how way leads on to way
I doubted if I should ever come back.

I shall be telling this with a sigh
Somewhere ages and ages hence:
Two roads diverged in a wood, and I,
I took the one less traveled by,
And that has made all the difference.

CAROL BANAYOS

When you decide to pursue your dreams and take the road less travelled you will be presented with opportunities. If the opportunity you are given, is an opportunity that will lead you to become more than you are now, take it. It won't be easy but it will be worth it.

CHAPTER 13 – EXERCISE

Check out www.carolbanayos.com/bonuses to complete the Chapter 13 Exercise for You are a Magnet.

CONCLUSION

In this book, I have tried to share with you my own experience from the start, where I was first given the jolt (although in my case, it took a number of jolts given the number of near-death experiences I have had). To the point where I decided that I must overcome the hurdles and curveballs of life while moving down the path that would take me to my ultimate goal. And right down to where I am in life today, at a point where I believe I am awake.

I am awake. I am consciously aware. I am no longer the lifeless soul or the zombie that I talked about at the start of my book. I am no longer just sitting at the wheel of life and letting someone else turn it left and right while I tag along. I have my hands on the wheel and my fingers wrapped very firmly around it. I control what I am doing. I have control over where I am headed in life. I have control over the speed at which I am progressing through this path. Quite simply, I have control. Let me tell you one thing: it feels amazing to be in charge. It feels amazing to know that you are the only one responsible for where you end up. It feels amazing to know that the equation of happiness is just a function of you yourself. It is not the function of societal conventions, what your mother says, what your father expects of you, the way others want you to behave, or what others think is acceptable.

I am at a point where the pen was given to me. I erased the old equation because the equation was faulty. The equation was faulty because everything should have been added up to lead to my happiness. But did it? No, it did not. My equation at that time included being in a relationship, but I was unhappy in that relationship. I felt used, exploited and cheated. So why was something that was making me feel all these negative emotions still a part of my equation? Should I have let it stay there or should I have had the strength to erase that from my life? Why was that person even part of my life when all I got was poison and hurt without any real love? I felt helpless, and needed control over my own emotions and life.

I am glad that I am at that point in life today where I had the power and courage to release negativity. Yes, it was not easy. Then again, it never really is, is it? If it were that easy, why would anyone else be having issues with it? What you really need to do is carry out a cost-benefit analysis. That is what I did. The first cost was that I was losing out on a companion. I no longer had someone to turn to in the darkness of the night to voice my fears. However, to be honest, I had not been able to do that for quite some time anyway. I had not been getting the support that I needed for a while now.

So what were the benefits? I was no longer going to be hurt and upset all the time. I was no longer going to be constantly worried about someone and what was going to happen next. I realized that my benefits were definitely greater than my costs, so I decided to eliminate this relationship from my life. In hindsight, even though the relationships were challenging, I am glad for the lessons it has taught me about myself and what I want and what I don't want.

The relationship was not the only faulty part in my equation of happiness. Things were still not adding up. There were a number of other things that I had still left in because there did not seem to be anything wrong with leaving them there. It is ironic that I am saying all of this today, because let me assure you that at one point in time I was blind enough to believe that I was actually going to get more happiness out of these things. Although I have already discussed this before, let me bring up this example again. I worked for almost six and a half years to get two degrees in majors that I thought would get me the right job that would allow me to earn the right kind of money. I thought it would take me where I wanted to be: a successful career. Well, surprise, surprise... It did not do that. So now that I come to think of it, I do not know whether it was really worth it to spend all that money and energy into working towards something that failed to provide me with what I had expected it to. Was it worth putting in all those nights cramming in the library? Was it worth all the extra stress and tension that I had to go through to make sure I was well prepared for the presentation, to make sure that my essay was formatted in the way that it was supposed to be, to make sure that every single deadline was being met? I think by now you all should have a pretty good idea of what my answer to that is going to be. So what should I have done? Well, I already had the degrees and there was no way in which I could possibly go back to the university and ask for my energy and happiness back. I could not really hand them the degrees and say, "Take this but give me back all the days I spent here." Unfortunately, this is not physically possible. What is possible, however, is that I now get to choose for myself. I get to sit back and think clearly about what I want from life, what I enjoy, and how it is going to help propel me in the direction of my ultimate goals. That is exactly what I have done.

I am now holding the reins; the ball is in my court. It is not always easy, but it feels awesome to know that I can handle it and that I am capable of dealing with whatever life throws my way. What makes it even easier for me to overcome the hurdles thrown at me along the way is that I know that overcoming them means that I get to be one step (or maybe even a few) closer to my ultimate goals. This makes me happy. Crossing every single hurdle is an achievement and an accomplishment in itself for me because I know that the distance between me and the point where I am destined to be is now decreasing rapidly. Trust me, this is a great feeling.

The purpose of my book was to inspire you to do the same. I do not know whether or not I have succeeded in doing this, but I am keeping my fingers crossed and hoping that I have succeeded. Even if one person decides to seek inspiration from me, I will consider myself to be successful because that would mean that there is one less zombie in this world and one more person who is alive in the truest sense. Throughout this book, you might have found a few pieces of advice scattered here and there as well. If nothing more, I hope that fragments of advice remain imprinted in your mind to eventually help you lead a more fulfilling and enriched life.

I will also summarize a few things here for your convenience. Perhaps some things escaped your mind as you were reading my ramblings. I would like to remind you that you need to figure out what YOU want in life. The world will tell you a hundred and one things. If possible, think back to the time you just graduated fresh out of college or university and everywhere you would go, people would ask you what you were doing next. Similarly, TV shows and magazines telling you how to dress, how to talk, walk and act. Basically, all these act as supposed guidelines to help you 'fit in.' I knew what I wanted to get into. For me, at least, that was a time full of confusion and a mixture of sadness and apprehension, so I would just mumble something here and there. More often than not, my mumbles would just be interrupted by someone patting me on the back and telling me that I should be doing this or doing that. For me, that was pretty annoying. I mean, I knew what I wanted and where I wanted to work. Now that you have read that, tell me what you think. Seems a little unfair, doesn't it? Did you like people giving you suggestions when you did not even ask them and telling you that this is the only right job or that is the only job that is acceptable for someone like you to opt for? I am guessing the answer is no. You probably wanted to be left to your own devices. You wanted time to figure out what you wanted to do. When you finally figured out what you wanted to be or what kind of job was right for you, I am sure that you felt much better, much more responsible, and much more relieved as well. So imagine what it would feel like if you extrapolate this and practice this in all aspects of your life. Let me tell you that it feels extremely fulfilling and amazing.

With this new responsibility and the challenge of making decisions on your own, you will undoubtedly face troubles as well. Still, try to give yourself a little credit for what you do manage to achieve. Sometimes, life will appear to be very scary and you wouldn't want to face it on your own. At times like these, it is okay to ask for help. Still, only ask people you know are willing to help you and provide you with the crutches you need to go through turbulent times. Learn to recognize who is just there for the joyride and who still remains next to your side when you are facing troubles. The latter is the person you want to stick to and the former is the kind of individual you need to avoid. You will have misconceptions, you will have fears and there will be traumas. But you cannot let these pull you down. You need to be very proactive in the way you approach them. When something bad happens, your first reaction should not be, "My life is ruined!" Your first reaction should be, "Hey, I was not expecting that, but let me see what I can do to fix this." When you actively face challenges instead of shying away from them, you will do yourself more good in the long run. As it usually goes; 'Just chuck it in your fuck it bucket.' On the other hand, if you just continue to blame others and the rest of the world and not do anything about the things you are struggling with, then your life will stay the same. There will be no change in your situation and you will continue to feel as hopeless as you were feeling before.

Whether you are at a stage where you feel you are already awake and consciously aware or are still journeying down the path that is going to lead to your awakening, remember that you are the only one who is responsible or can be held accountable for how your life turns out. You are in charge of your own strings, so do not be a puppet in the hands of someone else. Do not let anyone else manipulate you and do not let anyone else determine which direction you are going to take in your life. If you want to be at the place that you are destined to be at, stop being an extra in your own movie and start directing it as you see fit; let it be the most magnificent piece of work and beauty that you've ever seen. Remember that it all starts with waking the fuck up, while being consciously aware of your awakening. With this new awareness, anything is possible.

I will leave you with a poem from Elbert Hubbard.

Whenever you go out of doors, draw the chin in, carry the crown of the head high, and fill the lungs to the utmost; drink in the sunshine; greet your friends with a smile, and put soul into every handclasp. Do not fear being misunderstood and do not waste a minute thinking about your enemies. Try to fix firmly in your mind what you would like to do; and then without veering off direction, you will move straight in the goal. Keep your mind on the great and splendid things you would like to do and then, as the days go gliding by, you will find yourself unconsciously seizing upon the opportunities that are required for the fulfillment of your desire, just as the coral insect takes from the running tide the element it needs. Picture in your mind the able, earnest, useful person you desire to be, and the thought you hold is hourly transforming you into the particular individual... Thought is supreme. Preserve a right mental attitude. The attitude of courage, frankness, and good cheer. To think right is to create. All things come through desire and every sincere prayer is answered. We become like that on which our hearts are fixed. Whenever you go out of doors, draw the chin in, carry the crown of the head high. We are god in the chrysalis.

END NOTES

CHAPTER 1

Near-death experiences and rebirth
http://iands.org/about-ndes.html

http://www.livescience.com/6353-deadly-box-jellyfish.html

http://www.sapphyr.net/largegems/theawakening.htm

CHAPTER 3

Spirituality
Burkhardt, M. "Spirituality: An Analysis of The Concept," Holistic Nursing Practice, May 1989:60-77

http://endless-satsang.com/spiritual-enlightenment-spiritual-awakening.htm

CHAPTER 6

Health, Veganism, and the Many Benefits of Adopting a Plant-Based Diet
https://www.youtube.com/watch?v=30gEiweaAVQ

http://www.webmd.com/food-recipes/protein

https://www.vrg.org/nutrition/protein.php

Cowspiracy

CHAPTER 7

Resilience and inner strength
Krexy.com

ABOUT THE AUTHOR

Carol Banayos is a Self-Published Author, Entrepreneur, Creator, Life Coach, and Blogger. Carol is a graduate of the Asper School of Business from the University of Manitoba. She has a Bachelor of Commerce Honours Degree with a double major in Human Resources and Marketing. She also has a Bachelor of Arts Degree with a major in Psychology and a minor in Business Management, along with a Certification in Life, Executive Coaching, and Neuro Linguistic Programming (NLP).

Carol has always had a passion for helping others and pursued a career as a Human Resource Consultant with the Province of Manitoba. As a Human Resource Consultant, she provided on-going advice, guidance, and coaching on various human resource disciplines such as labour/employee relations; recruitment and retention; organizational design and classification.

After her third near death experience, she finally woke the fuck up and was now awakened on a higher level, while being consciously aware of the life that she was leading. This realization lead to a change in the life and career she wanted. Carol realized that she was conditioned, conforming to the norms of society. Therefore, she quit her secure position attained by working for seven years with the Province, to pursue her passion in real estate. This led her to life coaching and the writing of this book.

Carol's purpose and passion in life is to make this world a better place by having an inspiring and positive impact in people's lives by helping advise and guide them to realize and reach their fullest potential and to operate from their true authentic self. She is also passionate about educating and bringing awareness to veganism and adopting a plant-based diet.

GRAB YOUR FREE GIFT

Want to increase your awareness on each of the topics mentioned in this book?

Check out
www.carolbanayos.com/bonuses
to access your chapter exercises.

REVIEW THIS BOOK

If you like this book, please leave a 5-star review on my book page on Amazon.

Why not join the
"WAKE THE FUCK UP" movement
by spreading the word.

It will help more people and this world to Wake the Fuck Up.

www.ingramcontent.com/pod-product-compliance
Lightning Source LLC
Chambersburg PA
CBHW031710230426
43668CB00006B/170

9 780999 434086